PALMISTRY

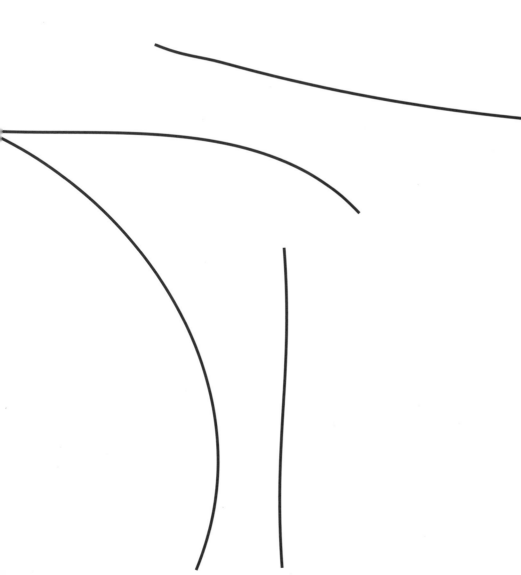

IMPRINT   First published in Great Britain in 1996
              by Hamlyn, an imprint of
              Reed International Books Limited
              Michelin House, 81 Fulham Road,
              London SW3 6RB
              and Auckland, Melbourne, Singapore and Toronto

JANE M^{c}INTOSH

KEITH MARTIN
ART DIRECTOR

BEN BARRETT   ISBN 0 600 58993 5
SENIOR DESIGNER

TANIA SARONY   A CIP catalogue record for this book is available from the
ILLUSTRATOR   British Library

PAUL WEBB   Printed in China
LINE ILLUSTRATOR

JOSEPHINE ALLUM
PRODUCTION CONTROLLER

JACKET DESIGN
AND ILLUSTRATION
BY BEN BARRETT

PALMISTRY

BETTINA LUXON

WITH

LINDA DEARSLEY

HAMLYN

CONTENTS

CONTENTS

INTRODUCTION

A few years ago a television documentary screened some extraordinary film of a foetus in the womb. Moved and amazed, the viewers watched breathtaking scenes of the tiny creature, this miniscule pre-child, drifting serenely through the amniotic fluid, eyes wide open, arms outstretched, feet gently paddling. Weeks before birth the infant appeared perfect in every detail and as it floated towards the camera its little fists unclenched and there, already deeply etched on its palms were the three major lines of the hand: the Life line, the Heart line and the Head line.

Many people, observing these lines in their own hands, believe that they are the result of wear and tear. They assume that the frequent folding and refolding of the skin as the hand clasps and unclasps cause the formation of these large "wrinkles". Yet this is not the case, as the documentary so graphically illustrated. The universal lines of the palm are present even before birth. Long before the hand is ever used at all, the distinctive markings are already in place. So what do they mean? Well, to a palmist it's no mystery. When those exquisite little hands came into view the night the documentary was screened, every palmist watching would have known exactly what she was looking at - nothing less than the blueprint of the child's future life and personality.

Centuries before brain scans and X-ray techniques were even dreamed of, palmists were building up a solid body of knowledge based on observation. They noticed that people with heavy thumbs tended to be quick tempered, people with pale, thinly marked palms usually lacked stamina, people with Heart lines that swung up between their first two fingers were often jealous types. Palmistry is believed to be over 3,000 years old, but unfortunately, somewhere along the line, it acquired a bad reputation. It was widely practised by gypsies from the East at a time when they were being persecuted and vilified.

Palmistry became associated with magic, witchcraft and dishonesty. It is only now that medical knowledge of the brain is advancing, that palmistry is once again beginning to be taken seriously. After 3,000 years, conventional scientists are catching up with palmists. They are starting to prove that mental activity can indeed be seen in the hand, just as palmists have said all along. These days doctors know that Downs syndrome can be detected in the hand of the subject. There is a typical Downs syndrome hand. It is short and broad with only two major lines where there are normally three. The Head and Heart lines are combined in one uncertain track in the centre of the palm. Then there is the difference between left- and righthanded people. Palmists have always said that lefthanded people tended to be original, artistic and musical, but up until now no one has been able to explain this.

Today we know that the brain is divided into two hemispheres. The left side of the brain, which controls the right side of the body, is related to speech and logical thought, while the right side of the brain, which controls the left side of the body, is related to the emotions and the understanding of shapes and space. Our brains are fed with a greater number of nerves on one side than on the other, and this determines whether we are right- or lefthanded.

So science bears out the findings of palmistry. Right- and lefthanded people are genuinely "wired" differently. Many lefthanded people are creative because they have more nerves that deal with the emotions than their righthanded friends.

There is nothing mysterious about palmistry. It makes sense and anyone can learn how to do it. It is simple, yet it can literally change your life, giving you valuable insights into your own character and that of others.

hand

shapes

HAND

The human hand is as individua

When I talk about different hand shapes people tend to look rather puzzled. A hand is a hand, they think, with four fingers and a thumb - so how can hands have different shapes? Then they might concede that some hands are small while others are large. Further prodding will get them to agree that some hands are thin while others are chunky, some have long fingers, others stubby - and before you know it the truth dawns. Hands are vastly different. It's true that unless something very unfortunate has occurred, they all have four fingers and a thumb, but the permutations possible within those basic constraints are quite extraordinary.

No human being has hands exactly the same as any other human being. In fact even your own hands, your left and your right, are not mirror images of each other. The human hand is as individual as the human brain that controls it, which is why palmistry can be so uncannily accurate. When you know what each tiny characteristic means, you can put together the unique personality before you like a fascinating jigsaw puzzle. When I have a new subject, I like to start by taking a look at the basic shape of his hands. This won't tell me his future, but it will give me a very good idea of the type of person he is. It's amazing how much the basic hand shape can reveal. And the exciting thing about a knowledge of the basic types is that it will enable you to form a rough opinion of the character of a complete stranger simply by glancing at his hands.

SHAPES
as the human brain

THE PALMIST
IN EACH OF US

Hands are of special interest to a palmist, but it's surprising how often we all "read hands" without even realizing it.

We speak of people being "open-handed" when they are generous, "tight-fisted" when they are mean and "light-fingered" when they are dishonest. Money "slips through our fingers" or we keep a "firm grip on the purse strings". We are "even-handed" when we're fair, "cack-handed" when we are clumsy. We often pay "back-handed compliments" and we frequently complain that "the left hand doesn't know what the right hand is doing".

Unconsciously we understand that hands are very revealing. We even put this knowledge into practice when we shake someone's hand. It is often said that you can judge a person by their handshake, and like many clichés, this is frequently true. Instinctively we recoil from a limp, damp handshake. We respond to a firm, elastic grip and we retire, somewhat bruised, from an iron hard bone-crusher.

Nine times out of ten those instinctive reactions are well founded. The flabby, lettuce-leaf grip suggests a lazy, lethargic temperament. The straightforward, strong grasp denotes an honest, alert brain, while the painful palm-mangler is likely to be a ruthless type of extreme energy who may even turn out to have a streak of cruelty.

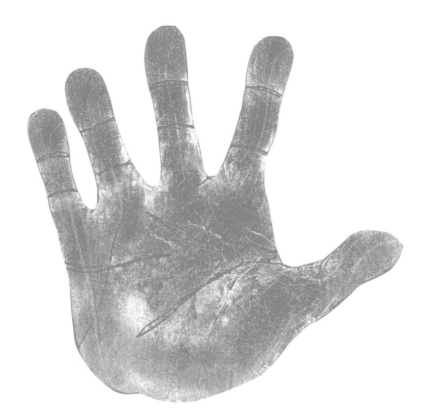

THE SPATULATE HAND

This is perhaps the easiest hand shape to identify. These hands are not elegant. There is sometimes an awkward, almost clumsy look about the spatulate hand. The palm is broad with a slight curve at the outside edge, and the whole hand seems to widen towards the fingers.

The fingertips themselves are particularly striking, since they splay out and flatten rather like a neat row of kitchen tools.

These hands belong to capable, open-minded outdoor lovers. They might not be the most imaginative of people but they are down-to-earth, versatile, practical and often very courageous.

Talented sportsmen and women tend to have spatulate hands, as do explorers and adventurers. These are people of action and energy who love nothing better than a challenge. They prefer to get on with things rather than waste time sitting around talking. They are adaptable and particularly good at open-air or manual work.

Despite their need for space, homelife is important to them and they complete domestic tasks with speed and efficiency. Their worst fate is to feel chained to a desk with a mountain of paperwork to complete.

Normally the owner of the spatulate hand is bluntly spoken with a good humoured disposition. However, he can be surprisingly changeable and display a real temper when things go wrong. Mechanical breakdowns and inadequate tools bring out the very worst in him.

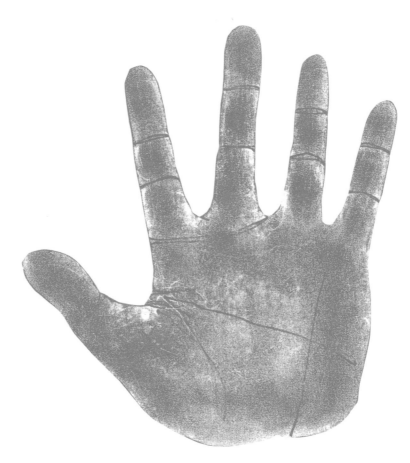

THE SQUARE HAND

This is another hand shape that is easy to identify. Neat and symmetrical, this hand has a straight, square palm and fingers that are neither too long nor too short, giving the whole hand a well balanced, boxy appearance.

The owner of the square hand is a dependable, law-abiding individual. The sort of person who needs order and discipline in his life. He will never stun his friends with wild and unpredictable behaviour but he will be much appreciated for his steady nature and cool good sense in a crisis.

People with square hands are natural conservatives in the non-political sense of the word and do well in professions that require sustained, consistent effort.

Lawyers, accountants and businessmen often have square hands; so do soldiers.

Yet despite their undoubted ability, people with square hands are often poor leaders. They do better as team players or lone workers. They don't really want the responsibility of sole command, although they will do their best if thrust into that position.

Most of all, these individuals loathe change and resist it whenever possible. They shine in familiar situations, but become uneasy and sometimes unreasonable when things around them change unexpectedly.

They are usually even-tempered and fair and enjoy a calm, well-organized home.

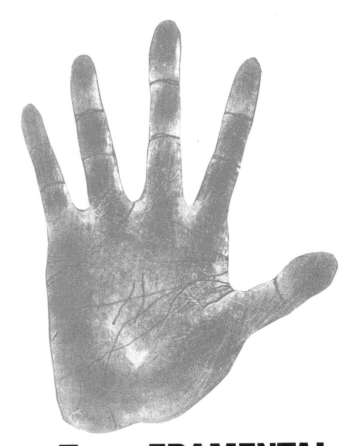

THE CONICAL OR TEMPERAMENTAL HAND

These attractive hands have long palms that taper slightly towards the fingers and long fingers that are full at the base and with pointed tips. The nails are usually ovoid.

Though these hands look very elegant, they often indicate a stormy passage through life.

Impulsive, quick thinking and vivacious, inspired by beauty in all its forms, the individual with conical hands can also be hopelessly changeable. He, or more often she, is frequently at the mercy of moods that reverse in an instant. Happy one moment, plunged into the depths of despair the next, they really don't understand why they should suffer in this way.

At best they are warm-hearted and sympathetic and would give away their last penny to a deserving cause. At worst they can be quick-tempered and selfish.

People with this hand shape are often drawn to religion in some form or another. They are not good in business and are more likely to let money slip away than to make it. Although they are not necessarily creative themselves they do best in fields where their love of beauty can be indulged. They are attracted to places where they can find lovely objects, such as craft and antique shops, art galleries and museums.

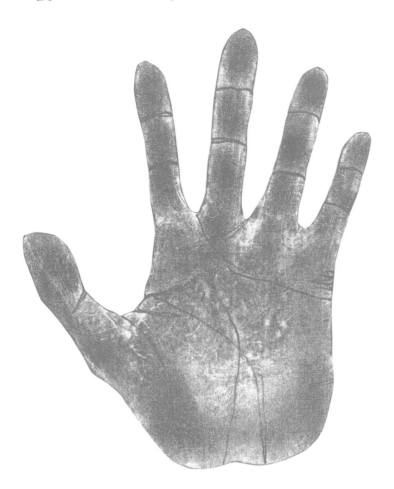

THE **PRACTICAL HAND**

Just as some hands are distinctly square, others can be described as almost perfectly rectangular. The palm is rectangular in shape. The fingers make another rectangle and the two together form one large rectangle.

I call this the practical hand because people with such hands have a knack of getting on with things efficiently and without fuss. They are peace-loving and law-abiding as well as intensely logical. These types will not be rushed and arrive at their decisions only after careful consideration.

They refuse to gloss over problems. They will continue to probe and analyse until they have got to the very heart of the matter, and then they set about putting things right in a calm, rational manner. This approach can be very irritating, but in the long run even short-fingered, impatient types can see that such thoroughness saves future headaches.

People with practical hands tend to do well in anything they undertake, but are particularly suited to long-term projects on a grand scale where a careful, measured approach is called for. Farming, planning, management, the law - any of these might appeal.

THE ARTISTIC HAND

People often believe that a thin narrow hand with long pointed fingers is the sign of the true artist, but this belief is quite mistaken.

The real artistic hand may be thin, but it is broad across the palm, with a pronounced curve on the outside edge. The fuller the curve, the more creative the owner is likely to be. The fingers tend to be long and flexible showing an openess to new ideas and the nails are frequently short and bitten. These artistic types are real nibblers and will chew away at pens, pencils or their own nails as they reflect upon their next creation.

Generally, the longer the fingers, the finer (in the sense of intricate) and more detailed will be the work they undertake. When the fingers are shorter the subject will often choose pottery, music or a bolder, more impressionistic style of painting as a means of self-expression.

The artistic type is not necessarily to be found isolated in a garret. People with artistic hands are often quite gregarious and use their talents in busy graphic design offices, photographers' studios or architects' practices.

Yet true to the old cliche, the artistic type is not usually good with money. Creation of a new project is more important to them than financial considerations. All too often someone else profits from their work. If by some fluke, they do make a fortune they are just as likely to lose it all again – because in the final analysis, they don't really care about money.

THE INTELLECTUAL/LONER

Here is a subject who wishes to be left alone. The loner feels oppressed by regulations and officialdom; the loner is oppressed by other people. He yearns to escape into a book.

This hand is extremely long and the fingers so strikingly elongated that the subject is bound to have been told at some point in his life that he ought to play the piano, though oddly enough, he very seldom does.

The skin of the hand is leathery and unyielding, the thumb stiff and strangely, considering the length of the fingers, only of average size. The whole hand appears pale.

Here is a person who is slow and thoughtful in everything he does: speech, movement, reactions. Nothing can be hurried. Introverted and probably shy, the owner of this type of hand finds human relationships difficult. He dreads parties and social gatherings and likes nothing better than to retire somewhere quiet with a good book.

The loner seeks out occupations that require little interaction with other people. This type makes good researchers, librarians and scientists and sometimes develops a strong and rewarding affinity for animals.

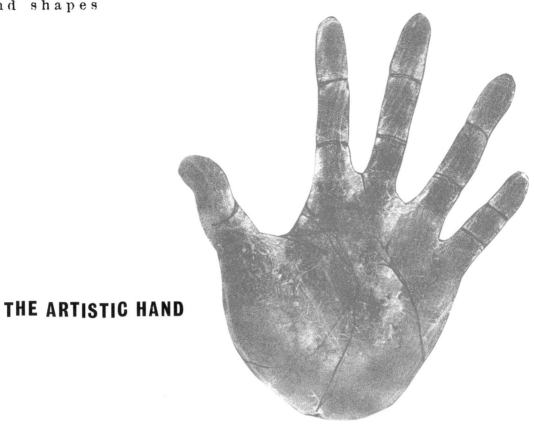

THE ARTISTIC HAND

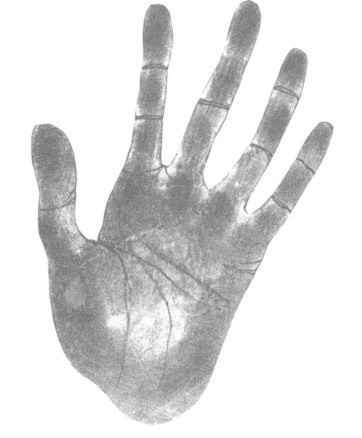

THE INTELLECTUAL / LONER

THE POINTED HAND

THE PRIMARY HAND

THE KNOTTY HAND

THE POINTED HAND

This is the hand most commonly mistaken for the artistic hand. It is long and very narrow with slender fingers bordering on boniness and elegant, pointed nails - the sort of hand with which portrait painters used to flatter their subjects.

Often it denotes a dreamer, a person lost in a world of his own who finds it difficult to come to terms with reality and the dreariness of practical matters.

Pointed hands look fragile and frequently denote people who are not robust. For this type, physical effort is sometimes a strain; a tendency to laziness is a frequent failing.

People with pointed hands are sensitive and occasionally even psychic, but hopeless with money. They love to be surrounded by beautiful things and a tidy, attractive home is very important to their wellbeing.

If at all possible people with pointed hands should marry into money and find someone to cosset them.

THE PRIMARY HAND

Short and broad, this hand has a large palm, thick, chunky fingers and a stout thumb. The nails are wider than they are long, the skin texture coarse and there are very few lines.

Just one look confirms that this hand was built for work and not elegance. People with primary hands tend to come from long lines of manual workers and are best suited to this type of work themselves.

Often very strong with a great deal of energy, they can endure hardship and even pain without complaint. They like to get on with the things that they are equipped to tackle and get impatient with a lot of academic work. They loathe petty regulations and filling in forms.

They like to keep things simple, but the desire to avoid complications can often misfire. People with primary hands tend to ignore rules that seem irrelevant and restrictive, and then they wonder why they so often land up in trouble.

Most of all the subject with the primary hand wishes to be left alone to get on with his life in peace.

THE KNOTTY HAND

The knotty hand is an interesting shape. All the joints are rounded and well developed but they have a healthy appearance not to be confused with the swollen look of arthritic hands.

Subjects with knotty hands are shrewd and astute. They have logical brains and like to grapple with intellectual puzzles. They are hardworking and inventive, and once they have made a decision they will stick to it. They tend to be intuitive although they would probably prefer to say that they have "gut" feelings that frequently turn out to be correct.

Unsentimental and inclined to be cautious, people with knotty hands often get too tied up in their work to notice relationships. Once you get through to them however, subjects with knotty hands make affectionate and loyal partners.

Business, financial affairs, the law - these are all areas in which the subject with knotty hands might like to work.

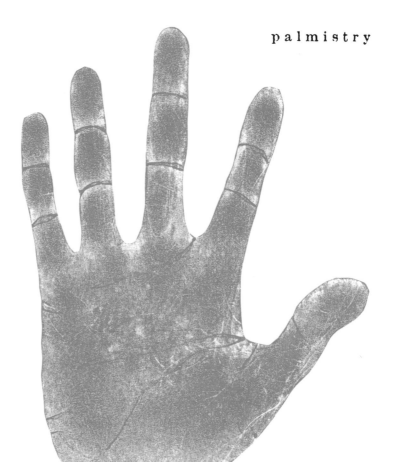

THE MIXED HAND

This hand shape is the one that confuses everybody. It doesn't appear to fall into any particular category but contains elements of several. But while the subject with the mixed hand may combine characteristics from other hand shapes, there is actually a "mixed hand" personality.

The subject tends to be versatile and adaptable and is good at solving problems by lateral thinking. Sometimes this very adaptability can be a drawback. People with mixed hands are often "Jacks of all trades" - they have a go at many things with varying degrees of success but become experts at none.

They are seldom bored because they have many interests, but they tend to be mental butterflies, skimming the surface of subjects, then moving on before they have mastered the topic in depth.

This doesn't mean that they are lacking intellectually. The subject with the mixed hand often has flashes of pure brilliance and many wonderful engineers, inventors and scientific researchers share this particular shape.

CASE HISTORY

THE SPATULATE HAND

Bill came to me with a career problem. He had recently been made redundant from his engineering job and since he was now in his early forties he feared that it would be difficult for him to find another post.

He had been good at his job but when I saw that he had spatulate hands I wondered if he had been in the right career at all. It turned out that what he enjoyed most was being out of doors. He lived for weekends when he could get out into his garden, which he had redesigned from scratch, putting in streams and water features, cleverly combining his engineering skills with his green fingers.

It didn't take a genius to work out where Bill's real enthusiasm lay, but even before he told me, I had seen it in his spatulate hands.

I suggested that he should change course, take up landscape gardening and be his own boss. That way he could make his hobby his work, and he wouldn't have to worry about his age.

After talking it over with his wife, Bill invested some of his redundancy pay in a landscape gardening course. Now he has established his own business, and has never been happier.

CASE HISTORY
CASE HISTORY

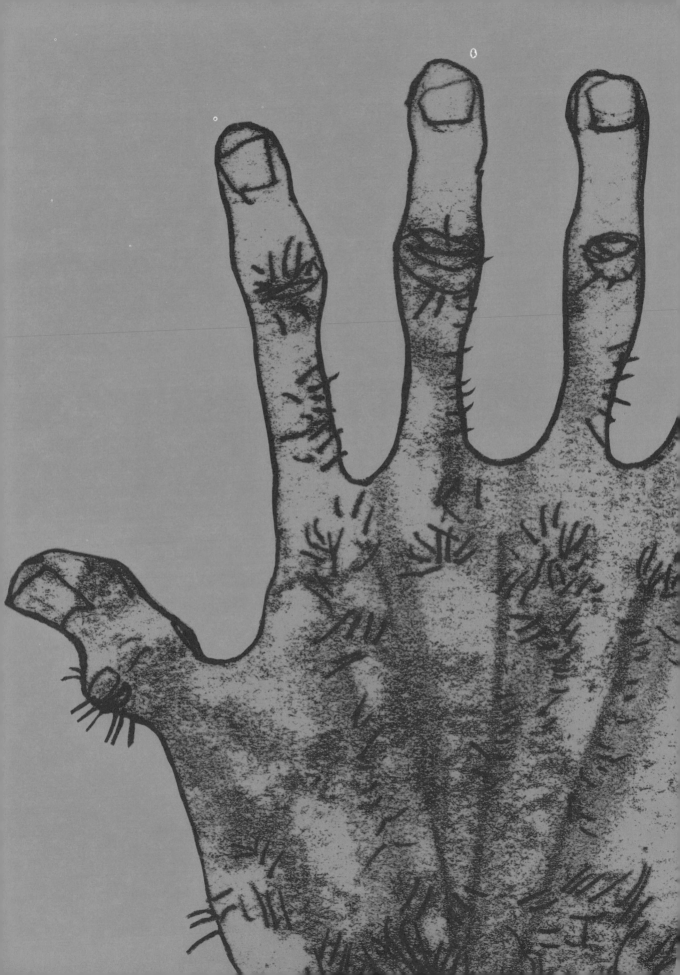

back of
hand

BACK OF HAND, KNUCKLES AND NAILS

Shape, texture, colour and the overall

Once you have identified the basic shape of the hand you are reading, the next step is to move a little closer. You have established the basic outline of the personality, and now you can begin to fill in a few broad details. There is still much the overall hand can tell you before you even glance at the palm and the lines contained within it.

The backs of the hands, the knuckles and the fingernails all hold vital insights into the character. Study them closely. Shape, texture, colour and the overall "feel" of the hand provide important clues.

Does the hand feel hard and muscular or soft and melting? Is the skin damp and clammy, hot or cold? Does the hand itself flex freely or is it stiff and unyielding?

Observe too how the subject uses her hands. Compulsive knuckle cracking is a sign that the subject is a highly strung individual with an inability to relax.

Finger-drummers are not necessarily bored or aggressive, but may well be bursting with nervous tension that has to find an outlet.

Nail-biters tend to be anxious souls, and so are people who pick at the quick of the nail and surrounding skin.

Sometimes you come across a hand in which the fingers are held closely together even when placed flat on a sheet of paper or table top. The owner of such a hand is likely to be a timid type with some worry or secret on their mind. Usually shy and sometimes insecure, the close-handed type tends to be careful with money and possessive with loved ones.

The open hand lies loosely on a flat surface with clear spaces showing between the fingers. The owner is likely to be confident, straightforward and rather careless with money. When the fingers are widely spaced this can indicate either extreme generosity or sometimes complete recklessness in financial matters. People with such hands find that money really does slip through their fingers, though they can't understand why.

For some reason many people are surprised to find that a palmist will even inspect their knuckles. Yet knuckles vary enormously from person to person. Study the knuckles as part of the back of the hand.

"feel" of the hand provide important clues.

Finally, make a thorough examination of your subject's fingernails. When the subject is a woman it's not always easy to tell the true colour of her nails because so many women wear nail varnish and even when they remove it, the remover itself often discolours the nail. However, when the nails are clean and free of all traces of cosmetic, the natural colour should be noted.

Doctors recognize that signs of illness can be detected in the fingernails. Brittle, ridged, concave nails point to iron deficiency or anaemia, and blue nails indicate respiratory problems.

Palmists have long checked nails for clues to health, but they also go a stage further. They see in the formation of the nail further insights into the personality within.

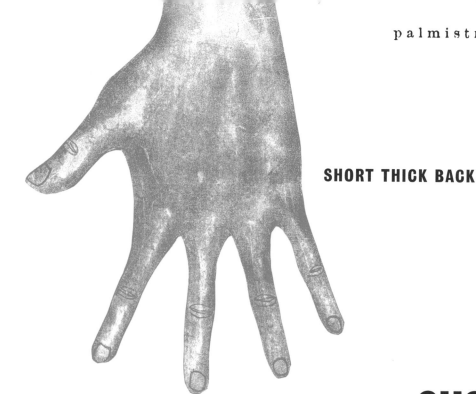

SHORT THICK BACK

SMOOTH BACKS

When the back of the hand is smooth and the skin texture fine and evenly coloured it reveals a lover of the beautiful things in life. These subjects enjoy lovely paintings, elegant clothes, the best china. They need comfort and attractive surroundings if they are to feel content.

SHORT THICK BACKS

Such hands are quite unusual and are often found in people who are highly intuitive. They sense when things are not what they seem and will not rest until they find out the truth. They tend to have big ideas but don't want to be both-ered with fiddly details and are prone to impetuous behaviour.

COLOUR AND "FEEL"

CLAMMY HANDS

Nobody enjoys shaking a clammy hand. Obviously we all perspire from time to time but some hands seem to be permanently damp. Such hands belong to anxious individuals who are always striving so hard to do the "right" thing, that they never quite manage to succeed.

COLD HANDS

The old saying "cold hands, warm heart" is well founded. Individuals with cold hands probably suffer from mild circula-tion problems but they are usually kind and well meaning.

HOT HANDS

People with hot hands are not necessarily less kind-hearted than those whose hands are always cold, but they are likely to frighten others away with their quick temper. Those brave enough to stand their ground may well detect a soft centre underneath the angry exterior.

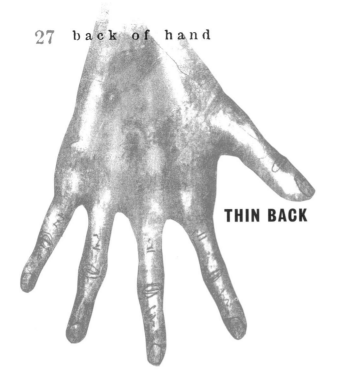

THIN BACK

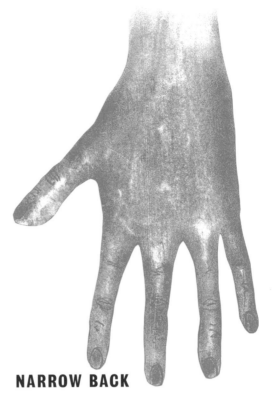

NARROW BACK

THIN BACKS

When the backs of the hands look thin and bony, the subject is likely to have a critical disposition which is linked to a quick mind. Original thinkers, sometimes artistic and usually bookworms, they are fascinated by the past and love antiques, ancient places and history.

NARROW BACKS

When the backs of the hands are very narrow it suggests a cool, undemonstrative nature. In negative hands the subject is likely to be coldhearted, but in a postive hand a narrow back simply indicates a difficulty in expressing emotion.

RED HANDS

When the whole hand including the palm is a definite red the subject is passionate, hot tempered, energetic and quite hard to handle. Such types tend to blow up like a volcano when annoyed and their rages can be quite terrifying. Afterwards however, they can't understand what all the fuss was about or why everyone else is upset.

SOFT PUDGY HANDS

Such hands, especially when the bases of the fingers are fleshy, belong to indolent, lethargic types. Yet surprisingly, considering their lack of energy in other areas, these hands also suggest a sensuous nature and a strong sexual appetite.

WHITE HANDS

A lack of stamina and possibly a tendency to anaemia is indicated when the hands are very pale. These subjects are sensitive and love beautiful things.

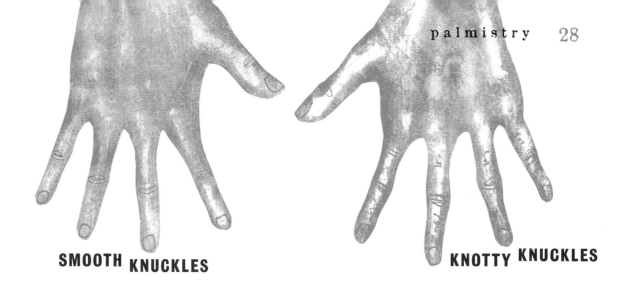

SMOOTH KNUCKLES

KNOTTY KNUCKLES

SMOOTH KNUCKLES

Sometimes the knuckles are smooth, flat and almost unnoticeable and there are very few creases in the skin over the joint. Such knuckles belong to a person who is easy-going, placid and hates stress. These individuals usually manage to have a calm passage through life.

KNOTTY KNUCKLES

Knuckles are known as knotty when they are raised and firm to the touch. Knotty knuckles denote a highly organized and logical brain and suggest that this person would do well in business.

TWO KNOTTY KNUCKLES

When the rest of the hand is smooth but the two middle fingers have knotty joints it indicates that the subject will have many obstacles to overcome before eventually finding success.

EXTREMELY KNOTTY KNUCKLES

Sometimes a hand with long fingers will display strikingly knotty, almost knobbly knuckles. When the knuckles are over-pronounced in this way it suggests a person who is obsessed with money. It makes no difference whether they are rich or poor. Money is their top priority.

HAIRY HAND WITH KNOTTY KNUCKLES

As long as the skin texture is not too coarse, this type of hand suggests an astute character with lots of new ideas. Such people are too shrewd to risk putting their innovations into practice themselves. They prefer to let others try them out first before taking the credit later.

KNUCKLES

NAILS

PINK NAILS

Pink is a good healthy colour, revealing an open mind and balanced outlook on life.

PINK NAILS WITH A WHITE MOON

People with these nails have a strong sense of justice, they insist on fair play and are sticklers for detail.

RED NAILS

Red indicates a hot-blooded, quick-tempered nature. People with red nails tend to speak before they think. They often regret their words later.

WHITE NAILS

When the nails are very pale it suggests the subject could be suffering from a vitamin and mineral deficiency. This type tends to be lethargic and lacking in energy

BLUE NAILS

Some sort of circulation problem is likely when the nails have a definite blue tinge. Subjects with blue nails should consult their doctors.

BITTEN NAILS

Normally bitten nails reveal a nervous, tense individual who worries over the slightest thing. However, when accompanied by an artistic hand shape, bitten nails may simply denote absentmindedness. Artistic types frequently nibble pens, paint brushes or possibly their own fingernails while they are dreaming up their next creation.

(BITTEN NAILS)

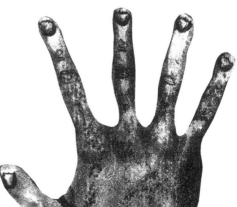

NAILS

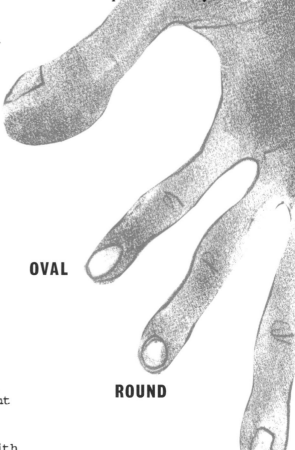

OVAL

ROUND

NARROW

OVAL NAILS

Perhaps the most visually attractive of all nail types, oval nails denote a sensitive, idealistic nature. Subjects with these nails expect the best from everyone and consequently suffer many disappointments when people fail to live up to their expectations.

ROUND NAILS

This may sound like an odd shape for a nail but in fact many nails are almost circular in appearance. Subjects with round nails tend to be vigorous, energetic and sexy. They are often quick-tempered but forget arguments as quickly as they start them.

NARROW NAILS

The subject with narrow nails tends to have a delicate constitution. Such people lack muscular strength, are often said to "live on their nerves" and are prone to colds, coughs and other minor ailments. However, they are highly intuitive. Psychics often have narrow nails.

OBLONG NAILS

True oblong nails are surprisingly rare. They are found in sweet natured, gentle people who hate confrontations of any kind. Arguments and discord make them feel ill and if they can't physically remove themselves from a quarrel, they will attempt to make peace.

CLAW-LIKE NAILS

Some women grow nails like talons in the belief that this looks feminine. But nails that could be claws suggest a cold, cruel nature. Such subjects are often highly ambitious and inclined to walk over anyone who stands in the way of their plans.

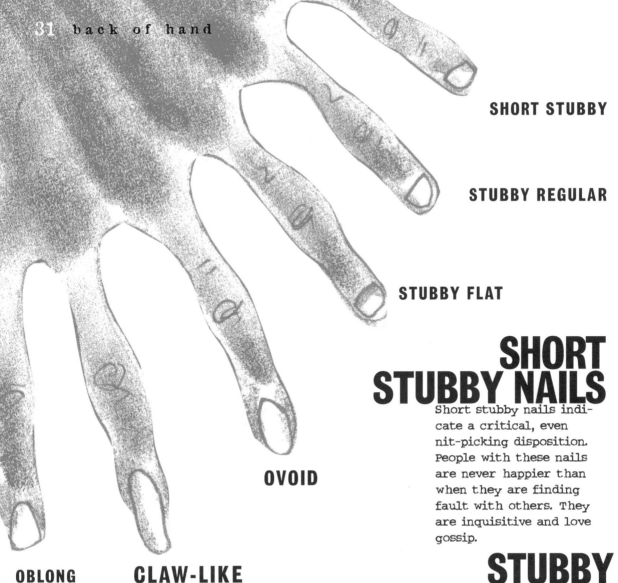

SHORT STUBBY

STUBBY REGULAR

STUBBY FLAT

OVOID

OBLONG   **CLAW-LIKE**

SHORT STUBBY NAILS

Short stubby nails indicate a critical, even nit-picking disposition. People with these nails are never happier than when they are finding fault with others. They are inquisitive and love gossip.

STUBBY REGULAR NAILS

When the nail is stubby and broad and curves round the fingertip the subject is likely to be blunt-spoken and frank. However, the width of the nail shows a broader mind and indicates someone unlikely to find fault with people who do things differently.

OVOID NAILS

Elongated nails belong to the dreamers of this world. They tend to wander around with their heads in the clouds, their imaginations working overtime. These subjects are open and frank in manner but they often lack energy or critical powers. They tend to get taken advantage of by others.

STUBBY FLAT NAILS

Sometimes the nails are so stubby that the skin seems to be growing right over the top. This is the sign of the true nosy parker, whose curiosity is so great that she can't help spying on neighbours and passers-by. No harm is meant, but this habit can be extremely annoying.

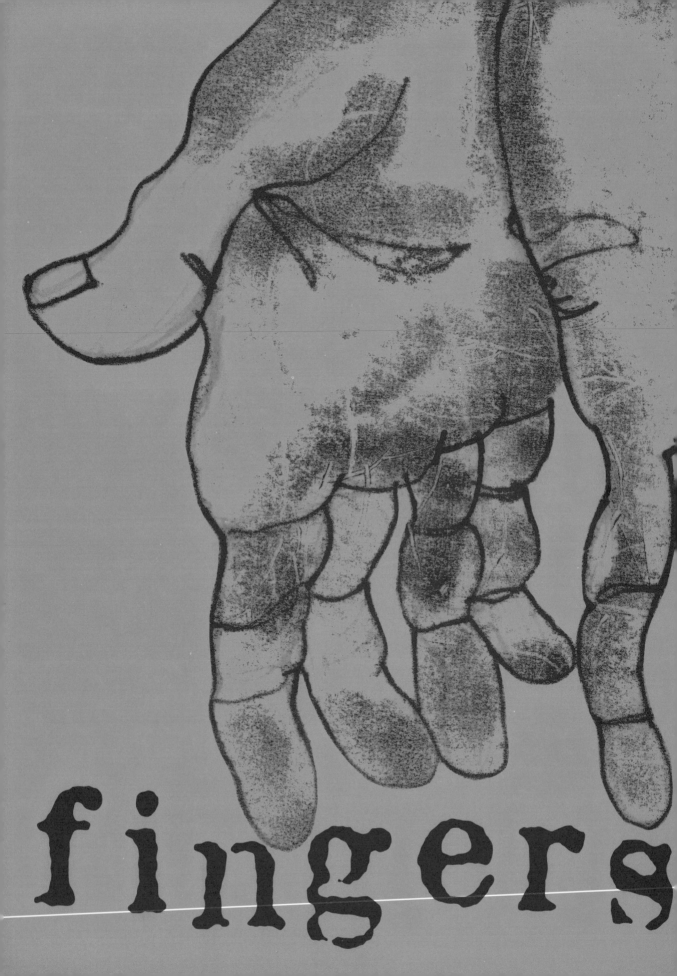

fingers

FINGERS

Instinctively, we all like to see a neat row of straight, nicely proportioned fingers. Not only do they appear attractive, they also suggest an attractive personality. Straight fingers are generally considered to be the outward manifestation of an honest, straightforward mind.
Crooked fingers that occur naturally, and not as the result of illness or injury, indicate the reverse. Criminals often have one or more twisted, bent digits and even if the subject doesn't engage in antisocial behaviour his mishappen fingers show that he is likely to prove untrustworthy or devious.
The genuine crooked finger is unappealing in appearance and unmistakable in character. It must not be confused with a finger that leans slightly towards one of its neighbours.

The flexibility of the fingers tells much

When a finger has a "tilt" in this way it suggests a minor weakness. Something is lacking in the character or some quality is desired. When the first finger (called the finger of Jupiter) veers towards the second finger (called the finger of Saturn) or even rests right on it, this indicates a lack of self-confidence. The finger seems to be leaning against its neighbour for support. Should the second finger of Saturn tilt towards the third finger (called the finger of Apollo, the Sun finger), which is influenced by the planet of success and material gain, it suggests a love of money and a desire to have more.

Short fingers belong to energetic, uncomplicated individuals. These types know what they want and prefer to go straight after it. They can't see any point in agonizing over decisions or weighing up pros and cons. Impulsive, quick thinking and endowed with strong sexual appetites, especially if their fingers are fleshy at the bases, they are the doers of the world.

Sometimes these qualities can work against them. Short-fingered individuals are not usually the most tactful of people. They don't waste time couching their thoughts in careful language and for this reason they sometimes upset their friends and colleagues. They can be impatient, irritable and intolerant and sometimes their desire for immediate action leads them to make mistakes.

The one thing a person with long fingers can't be accused of is rushing into things. Unlike their short-fingered friends, individuals with long fingers prefer to take their time and study a project from every angle before committing themselves. They never speak before they think, positively relish detail, and are thorough in everything they do. Affable and gregarious, this type makes friends easily and rarely falls out.

On the negative side, long-fingered people often miss opportunities because they spend so long making up their minds about which course of action to take. Excessively long fingers suggest a withdrawn character who prefers mental pursuits to physical pleasures. This type doesn't usually mix well with others and are happiest when buried deep in some highly detailed, painstaking task.

The flexibility of the fingers tells much about flexibility of character. The more supple the fingers, the more adaptable the personality. The fingertips provide further clues. Most fingertips are endowed with fleshy little pads. When these pads feel soft and yielding to the touch it shows that the subject is a softhearted, unassertive person who must guard against being put upon. When the pads feel firm and springy, the subject is likely to be independent, self-aware and impatient of orders or criticism. People with firm fingertips such as these would do well to be self-employed since they need to feel in control and dislike authority.

about flexibility of character.

Occasionally you find fingers that are so hard and bony they scarcely seem to have pads at all. These belong to ruthless individuals who would stop at nothing to get what they want. Nobody pushes this type around. Nobody would dare.

Before moving on to look in detail at the individual fingers, examine the line they make as they join the palm. Does it form a gentle curve sloping downhill towards the fourth finger (the finger of Mercury)? Or does it go straight across from one side of the palm to the other?

The most common formation is the gentle curve. This shows that the subject has had to work hard to make his own way in life. The straight line formation is much more rare. When the fingers all start from the same place on the palm it is a sign that the subject has had a very good start in life. These types are usually from wealthy families and may have inherited fortunes or have been able to walk into interesting, lucrative careers thanks to the influence of relatives or friends.

FIRST FINGER OF JUPITER

We tend to describe the fingers as long, short or normal, taking the second finger, the finger of Saturn, as the base line. The normal length of the first finger of Jupiter is about four-fifths the length of Saturn.

JUPITER

SATURN

NORMAL FINGER OF JUPITER

The subject is confident, has a healthy sense of self and treats others with respect.

LONG FINGER OF JUPITER

Sometimes the first finger of Jupiter is almost as long as the second finger of Saturn. This is indicative of great confidence and a tendency to dominate others. Born leaders have this type of finger, but if they can't find the right outlet for their talents, their leadership qualities can deteriorate into bossiness.

SHORT FINGER OF JUPITER

Timidity is the keynote here. These subjects are lacking in confidence. They fail to stand up for themselves and are often branded as cowards. They can be very selfish too, but only because they are so busy worrying about their own inadequacies that they fail to notice other people.

When the first finger of Jupiter is shorter than the third finger of Apollo, this suggests a full-blown inferiority complex.

LOW-SET FINGER OF JUPITER

Sometimes the finger of Jupiter is set low down in the palm, below the level of the other fingers. This is a good sign suggesting abundant energy and self-discipline.

Note: Occasionally I have come across a small line encircling the base of the first finger of Jupiter. This is a very unusual sign and indicates a powerful interest in the occult.

THE SECOND FINGER OF SATURN

This is normally the longest finger on the hand, although occasionally, as previously seen, a long finger of Jupiter can almost match it. I have also seen a third finger of Apollo reach similar lengths. This is a rare sign and usually found in the hands of millionaires or those destined to become millionaires.

NORMAL FINGER OF SATURN

The subject is cheerful and in control of his emotions. Providing the thumb is also well balanced, he has a well adjusted temperament.

LONG FINGER OF SATURN

Emotions often prove difficult for subjects with long Saturn fingers. Serious and inclined to melancholy, these types are plagued by mood swings. If the finger is excessively long it suggests a morbid outlook.

SHORT FINGER OF SATURN

Individuals with short Saturn fingers are never satisfied. They tend to be immature, dislike responsibility and have high expectations, which they can't meet. They suffer frequent disappointments, and tend to blame their misfortune on others.

MILLIONAIRE'S HAND

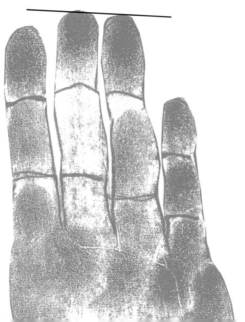

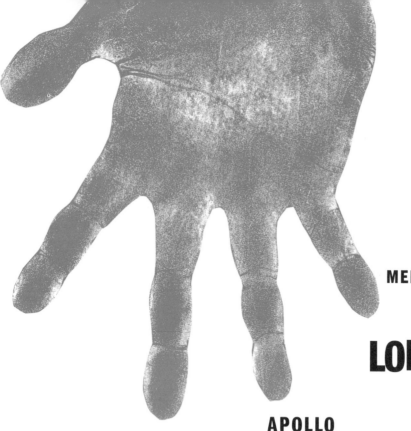

MERCURY

APOLLO

LONGFINGER OF APOLLO

When this finger is long it suggests a highly ambitious individual who is likely to go far in her career. Money seems to gravitate to these types and they are prepared to take risks to advance themselves. Should the finger be excessively long, the subject is likely to be a gambler. There may be spectacular gains, but also spectacular losses.

THE THIRD FINGER OF APOLLO

Traditionally this finger is associated with art, careers and worldly success. It normally comes three quarters of the way up the second finger of Saturn.

NORMAL FINGER OF APOLLO

A normal finger of Apollo shows an appreciation of beauty, art and culture as well as a keen interest in career and money matters.

SHORT FINGER OF APOLLO

You would not find subjects with such fingers in an art gallery or museum, or at least not by choice. They prefer more down-to-earth pursuits and are quite unmoved by beauty. They would dearly like to succeed in their careers but lack real ambition.

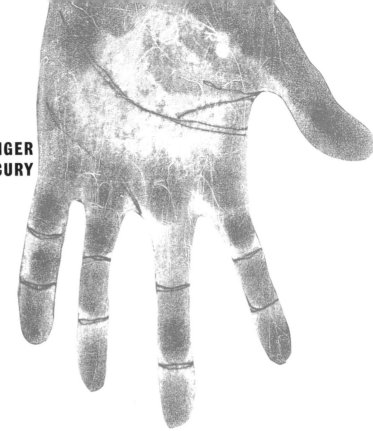

**THICK FINGER
OF MERCURY**

THE FOURTH FINGER OF MERCURY

The fourth finger, the little finger, is typically associated with communication, both in personal relationships and in career matters. Should this finger be noticeably thicker than the others it suggests an argumentative nature. This type of person frequently fails to get on with friends and workmates because she can't help disagreeing with them.

This finger usually reaches seven-tenths of the way up the second finger of Saturn.

SHORT FINGER OF MERCURY

The subject with the short finger of Mercury often knows what he wants to say but can't quite articulate it. He frequently puts his foot in it, or says something sarcastic when he intended to make a joke.

NORMAL FINGER OF MERCURY

When the little finger is of normal length it suggests a tactful individual who gets on well with others and is able to speak up for herself when the need arises.

LONG FINGER OF MERCURY

These are the types who have kissed the Blarney stone. Articulate, diplomatic and ingenious, they are never lost for words. They are brilliant salesmen, politicians and businessmen and can hold enormous power over others.

CROOKED FINGERS

On several occasions in the past I have been asked by employers in small firms to help find the identity of a dishonest member of staff. This is a surprisingly common problem and one that is notoriously difficult to solve. There is often no evidence to go on and the employer risks giving grave offence, which could even lead to legal action, if he accuses the wrong person. Yet the matter cannot be ignored. I have known huge losses running into thousands of pounds.

This is a situation that requires very delicate and discreet handling. Usually I am invited along to the office in an informal capacity. There I wander around, chatting to the staff and providing a little entertainment by giving mini-palm readings, which are always popular. This is fun, but at the same time it gives me the opportunity to check hands for tell-tale signs of dishonesty.

In every case I've investigated, I've found someone, and on one occasion two people, with crooked fingers. Naturally you can't accuse someone of a crime merely because you don't like the look of their fingers, but I've advised the employer which

member of staff to watch. Invariably the person with the bent fingers turns out to be the culprit.

Misshapen fingers don't always mean criminal tendencies. I came across a woman recently who was upsetting her colleagues for quite a different reason.

Sally was very smart and pleasant in appearance, but her personality jarred. Though she wasn't prepared to help anyone else, she frequently asked her colleagues to do her enormous favours. She wheedled, pleaded and resorted to devious lies to get her own way, and if anyone refused to do as she wanted, she turned on them viciously.

It was her workmate Charlotte who told me about Sally.

"Now she's thinking of starting her own business and she wants me to join her," said Charlotte. "I've got some savings and Sally needs to raise more money to get started. I don't really like her, but it's a good idea. What do you think, Bettina?" We had lunch together then I went back to the office with Charlotte, ostensibly to see where she worked. There I met Sally. Outwardly she was charming, and asked me to read her palm. She

hoped to hear that her business was going to be a great success.

In fact, all the signs suggested that it would succeed, but nevertheless I advised Charlotte not to get involved in any way and certainly not to invest her savings in the project.

Sally's fingers were very hard and extremely bony. Added to that both her first finger of Jupiter and her fourth finger of Mercury were twisted in a most peculiar way. They both bent towards the second finger of Saturn and then started to lean back again.

I realized that Sally was ruthless, sly and devious in her dealings with other people. She expected people to give without limit yet was quite oblivious to her own faults. If something went wrong, everyone else was always to blame.

Anyone who went into partnership with Sally would have a very bad time indeed. What's more, Sally would always manage, by fair means or foul, to turn every situation to her own advantage. Sally would certainly profit from her business. The chances were that Charlotte would not.

CASE HISTORY

LONG FINGER OF JUPITER

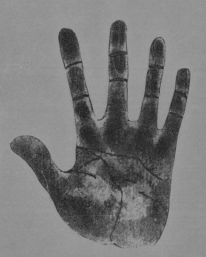

I came across another interesting case at an office party one year. A group of secretaries, in a very giggly mood after a few glasses of Christmas punch, challenged me to take a look at the hands of their boss. He was an ogre, they insisted: quite unbearable. He stomped around issuing orders and demanding instant obedience. Everyone was frightened of him.

Mr X sounded a daunting prospect indeed. Fortunately, despite his forbidding exterior, he had excellent manners and didn't flay me alive for approaching him. And when I looked at his hands I saw that under that authoritarian façade he was a pussycat: warm-hearted, sentimental and genuinely caring. Despite his bluster he hated to see people hurt and did his best to protect his staff.

One thing that was immediately apparent, however, was his long first finger of Jupiter. Here was a man born to lead. Further probing uncovered the real problem. Although Mr X was head of his department, another manager had been appointed over his head to coordinate the work of several departments, including that of Mr X. Mr X felt undermined now that decisions were out of his hands.

Unable to take a genuine lead, he vented his frustration in acts of bossiness, exercising every bit of authority that was left to him.

For someone like Mr X it was an intolerable situation, and I suggested he think about changing his job if possible. A few months later I heard he had done just that. What's more, he took his old secretary with him to his new company. There he was a changed man, she confided to me afterwards. Now that he had real decisions to take, genuine control to exercise, he no longer shouted and raged. In fact, oddly enough he was the most popular manager in the company.

CASE HISTORY

CASE HISTORY

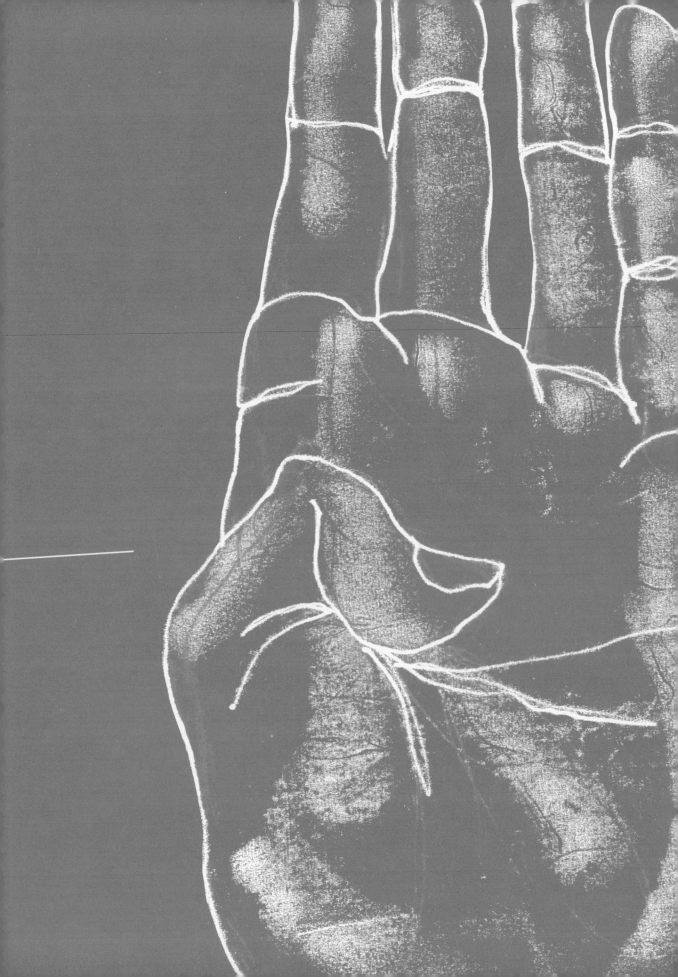

thumbs

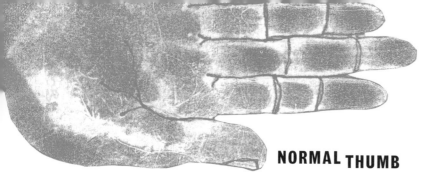

NORMAL THUMB

THUMBS

"I don't know what's the matter with me today," people often say, "I'm all fingers and thumbs." What they actually mean, of course, is that they are being unusually clumsy. It's a strange choice of expression, when you think about it. After all, imagine how much more clumsy we would be without fingers and thumbs. Nevetheless we understand what is meant and the familiarity of the old saying only underlines the importance of the digits. Many scientists believe that it is the human hand alone, with its wonderfully dexterous fingers and thumb, that marks us out from other animals and has allowed man to become the dominant species.

Whatever the truth of this theory, there is no doubt that palmists attach great importance to fingers and thumbs. Each finger is believed to be influenced by the qualities attributed to certain planets - Jupiter, Saturn, Apollo (or the Sun) and Mercury - and is named after them. The thumb stands alone, bearing no special name. Perhaps this is because the thumb draws its influence not from some outside force, but from within. The thumb represents the true spirit of the individual subject - her will and her unique sense of self. Of all the digits palmists regard the thumb as the most significant, and it is extraordinary how closely a person's thumb reflects his state of mind.

A friend of mine was going through a period of depression recently and she suddenly noticed that when she was sitting quietly her thumb automatically curled into the palm of her hand. Of course she could lift it out again whenever she wished but as soon as she stopped concentrating and thought of something else, her thumb would slip back under her fingers. She was so miserable that her confidence and self-esteem seemed to have melted away. She didn't care what happened to her, she couldn't make decisions, she seemed to have lost her very will. All of this could be seen in the position of her thumb.

Fortunately she began to improve and amazingly enough, as she did so, so her thumb began to reappear quite involuntarily from inside her hand. At last when she was completely recovered it regained its former place, held confidently high on the outside of her palm.

The fascinating thing about this episode was that it was entirely unconscious. Even when she noticed what was happening my friend was unable to control it for more than a few minutes at a time. Only when she was genuinely healed inside would the thumb resume its former healthy position.

The significance of the thumb can also be seen in newborn babies. Immediately after birth when the tiny infant is totally dependent on others and hardly knows where the outside world ends and its own body begins, its hands are held in tight little fists, thumbs clamped firmly inside, will dormant.

The thumb represents the true spirit of the individual - her unique sense of self

Yet as the months pass and the baby gradually develops a mind and a temper of its own, the hands unclasp and the thumb comes out into the open.

In later life the thumb changes position with changing circumstances. When elderly people become senile and dependent on others, their thumbs tend to retreat back inside the palm. Something similar happens to the very sick if they lose the will to live.

I have even noticed this phenomenon in epileptics. Just before a seizure the thumb abruptly folds away as if the body has recognized that it is about to lose control. Once the fit is over the thumb reappears as if nothing has happened. Bearing all this in mind, it is not surprising that palmists check thumbs with particular care.

Once you have observed the way the subject holds his thumb the next step is to note the shape, size and position on the hand. Then you can move on to the individual bones or phalanges.

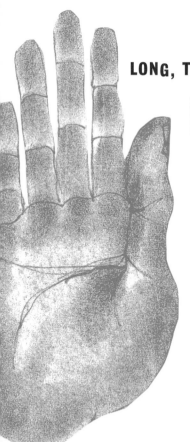

LONG, THIN THUMB

LONG THUMB

People with long thumbs are the types whose heads rule their hearts. Confident and in control, they prefer to give orders rather than to take them. They tend to be practical, logical and analytical in their approach. If they promise to do something, they will certainly do it. They appear daunting and cool to short-thumbed folk, but often their efficient exterior masks a warm heart.

THIN THUMB

This is the reverse of the cushioned thumb. Thin thumbs suggest a struggle to succeed. The individual with such a thumb may do very well indeed but often at great personal sacrifice. These types have had little time for fun and relaxation and would do well to allow a little frivolity into their lives.

SHORT THUMB

Short thumbs suggest some fundamental flaw or weakness in the character. This does not mean that the subject is an unpleasant person, just that they will have to work hard to overcome an unfortunate trait that could hinder their chances of success. Short-thumbed subjects tend to be full of big ideas but lack the necessary willpower to put them into action. They are sentimental and find it difficult to compete with other people. They can be nervous and lacking in confidence and need to work on building their self-esteem.

SHORT, CUSHIONED THUMB

CUSHIONED THUMB

Sometimes the tip of the thumb is well cushioned with flesh. This indicates that life has been kind to these subjects. They have made headway with little effort and have been able to concentrate heavily on their own pleasures.

LOW-SET THUMB

Chimpanzees, whose hands bear a strong resemblance to those of man, tend to have thumbs that are set very low down on their hands. This shows their comparative lack of willpower, ambition and concentration. Occasionally a human being will have a similar thumb. This suggests a similar lack of will and concentration but before reaching a firm conclusion the palmist must also study the Head line in the palm.

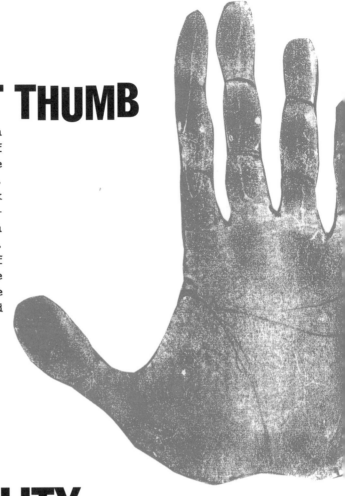

THUMB FLEXIBILITY

If you bend the thumb gently backwards, away from the hand, you will notice one of two things. Either the digit will feel stiff and unyielding, noticeably resisting the movement or it will rock easily backwards with a springy, supple sensation.

The unyielding thumb is known as "inflexible", while the supple thumb is described as "flexible", for obvious reasons.

The inflexible thumb tends to look straight and possibly rigid. This type of thumb belongs to a person who is reliable, fair-minded and steady in approach. While not exactly cautious, this person cannot be accused of impetuous behaviour. She knows her own mind, won't change it without a great deal of thought, and can be quite opinionated at times.

The flexible thumb is very different, reflecting a flexible approach in life. This type of thumb indicates an adaptable, gregarious person who will bend over backwards to reach agreement with others. He will not necessarily change his views when in the company of people who think differently, but he will endeavour to find a compromise, accentuating areas of agreement and down-playing areas of conflict.

The individual with the flexible thumb is a useful employee because he is so adaptable that he can slot into many different posts and is guaranteed to get on with his new colleagues when he does so. The only problem is that, amicable as he is, you never really know where you stand with him.

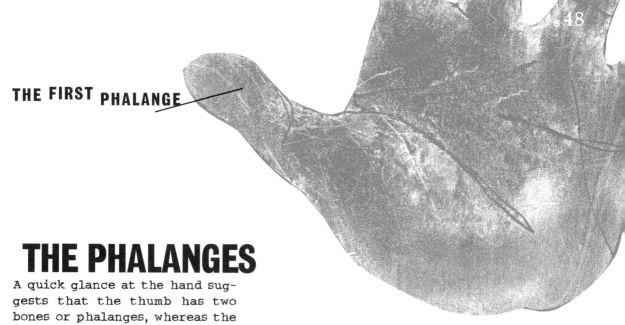

THE FIRST PHALANGE

THE PHALANGES

A quick glance at the hand suggests that the thumb has two bones or phalanges, whereas the other fingers have three. Yet look more closely and you will realize that the joint below the second phalange of the thumb, the joint that forms the side of the hand, is in fact the third phalange. When studying the thumb, all three phalanges must be considered.

THE FIRST PHALANGE

This is the phalange at the top of the thumb, the nailbearing section. This stands for willpower and determination - "stickability", as some might put it. Ideally the first two phalanges should be the same size, showing a good mental balance, but if the first phalange is longer than the second it suggests a nature that is wilful to the point of obstinacy.

If the joint is very overdeveloped it indicates someone who rides roughshod over others in her determination to get her own way. A heavy, almost bulbous joint is a very worrying sign. It shows a dangerous temper, a very short fuse and an inability to accept that one can't always have what one wants. This type of thumb is often found on the hands of violent criminals and murderers.

Sometimes the first phalange is short and wispy looking. In this case the subject lacks willpower and will rarely find the determination and persistence to carry a good idea through to a successful conclusion.

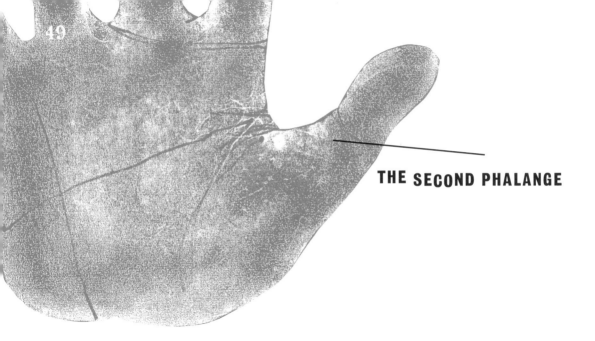

THE SECOND PHALANGE

THE SECOND PHALANGE

The second phalange is associated with reason, logic and analytical thought. When it is the same length as the first phalange and both are well developed, not thin, insignificant little joints, then the subject is likely to have a good balance between logical thought and willpower. She will have plenty of clever plans and the determination to put them into action.

Should the second phalange be longer than the first it suggests a good intellect in danger of being wasted, because the subject gives up too easily when he might accomplish many things.

When the second phalange is short and poorly developed, the subject tends to lack reasoning power and is often accused of being illogical. Unable to analyse problems, he tends to base decisions on emotional responses or "gut reactions". Sometimes this approach is surprisingly successful, but often it creates more problems than it solves and the subject is likely to stagger from crisis to crisis wondering why everything seems to go wrong.

The second phalange often has a slightly "waisted" appearance, it curves in under the first phalange before sweeping out again to the third. This is an indication of tact and diplomacy. People with waisted thumbs very seldom put their foot in it. They seem to know instinctively how to handle most situations.

When the thumb is heavily waisted however, this is not a good sign. It suggests a sly, cunning mind. The subject may be trustworthy, but on the other hand he may not. It depends what suits him at the time.

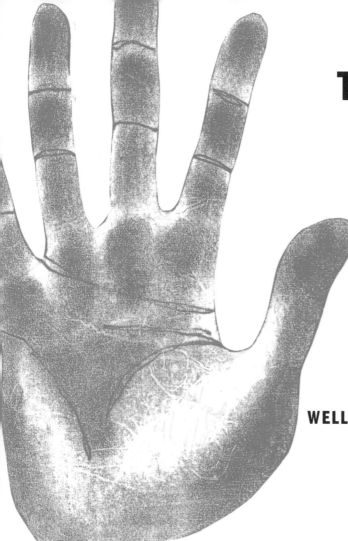

THE THIRD PHALANGE OR MOUNT OF VENUS

The thumb is the only digit that has a "mount" as its third phalange. A mount is a raised, cushiony area on the palm. The third phalange of the thumb is known as the Mount of Venus and it is situated at the base of the thumb, behind the Life line.

Whereas the first two phalanges relate to will and reasoning, the Mount of Venus deals, as its name suggests, with affection and emotion.

WELL-DEVELOPED MOUNT OF VENUS

EXCESSIVELY DEVELOPED MOUNT OF VENUS

Sometimes this mount is excessively developed. When it seems to dominate the hand and looks generally out of proportion, it suggests a person who is rather vain and unstable. These types are more in love with themselves than others and for this reason have difficulty in communicating. They believe other people are always responsible for their problems. They cannot conceive that they themselves could ever be at fault.

WELL-DEVELOPED MOUNT OF VENUS

Ideally the mount is raised, rounded and full and has a pleasantly cushioned feel when gently pressed. This suggests an affectionate, kindhearted individual who is thoughtful and tolerant of others. Subjects with such mounts tend to love music, animals and family life. They make friends easily and have the capacity to be both tender and passionate in bed.

FLAT, NARROW MOUNT OF VENUS

When the mount is so flat that it can scarcely be called a mount at all and the area within the Life line is very narrow, it suggests a coldhearted individual with very little feeling for other people. These are the types who would not do a good turn for others unless there was some powerful incentive, usually financial. Unable to appreciate beauty, art or the finer things in life, they often appear mean-spirited and unhappy. When such a mount has a hard, leathery feel it could even suggest that the subject has criminal tendencies.

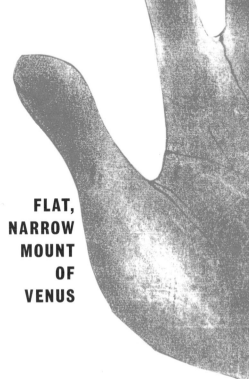

FLAT, NARROW MOUNT OF VENUS

FLABBY MOUNT OF VENUS

Occasionally the Mount of Venus has a flabby, over-yielding quality. In this case the subject may be generous and sympathetic, but only as long as no effort on her part is required. She is sensuous and sexy and enjoys physical pleasures of many kinds but, above all, she is lazy, and this inbuilt indolence overcomes everything else. These types might accomplish many things but they just can't summon up the energy to get started.

GRILLED MOUNT OF VENUS

When the Mount of Venus is crisscrossed with little lines and the whole hand is red it suggests the passionate nature of someone who needs a great deal of sexual variety. Often selfish in bed, these types may possess great charm out of it and have no trouble finding new partners. They may be fun for a while, but long term commitments are almost impossible for them to make. These individuals are born to break their marriage vows.

CASE HISTORY
THE VIOLENT THUMB

Some time ago a woman came to see me because she was very worried about her teenage son. Kevin was a goodlooking boy of about 15 with a shy smile and floppy hair that fell across his eyes.

You would have thought that life would soon open up all sorts of marvellous opportunities for such a boy. But his mother explained that Kevin was about to be expelled from school. The teachers couldn't control him and neither could she. As for his father - he had walked out years ago.

My first instinct was that everyone was being unfair to Kevin. He had had a difficult start in life and now he was being made a scapegoat. It happens all the time. But when I looked at Kevin's hand I saw that he had short, heavy thumbs with bulbous tips. The second phalanges were particularly undersized.

I realized that we had a serious problem here. Kevin lacked reasoning ability, so he responded emotionally to every situation. The longer, heavier first phalange revealed a quick temper leading to instant fury if Kevin was denied his own way, and that bulbous tip betrayed a violent streak. In short, Kevin was a human time bomb. He found offence wherever he went and responded to it with aggression.

I talked to his mother of the need for Kevin to control his temper, to back off and cool down for a while when things annoyed him, to think before he lashed out.

But I knew I was probably wasting my breath. Poor Kevin lacked the intellect to see the sense in what I was saying and the power to put it into action.

Kevin was not a bad boy and he didn't mean any harm. But sadly he was expelled from school for fighting, and from then on he drifted into crime. By the time he was 19 he was in prison.

CASE HISTORY
CASE HISTORY

CASE HISTORY
SENSUOUS MOUNT OF VENUS

Evelyn and her husband Max came to see me when they were having difficulties in their marriage. Evelyn thought Max was having an affair. Max denied it. He was a builder and he often worked late, frequently accepting jobs away from home. According to him, Evelyn was simply getting jealous because she was on her own a lot.

Yet I knew as soon as I looked at his hand that he wasn't telling the truth. Perhaps he wasn't having an affair just at that moment, but the red, heavily lined Mount of Venus told me that Max couldn't be faithful to one person. He was a sensuous man who needed a variety of partners in order to feel satisfied. He was quite unable to stay true to Evelyn and he had probably had dozens of affairs during their marriage.

Oddly enough, many marriages survive this type of behaviour as long as the faithful partner accepts the nature of the unfaithful partner. Max's unfaithfulness was no reflection on his wife and the chances are that in his own way, he did genuinely love her.

The strange thing is that individuals with this type of Mount of Venus tend to run out of steam sexually, often before they reach fifty. From then on they make reliable spouses, although the danger is that even their sexual feelings for their partner will have disappeared.

I was as tactful as I could be towards Evelyn and Max, and they went off to try to mend their marriage. In their case it didn't work. Max did lose his apppetite for sexual adventures eventually, just as his hand showed that he would. Unfortunately for him, long before this happened, Evelyn lost patience and left him for another man.

Now Evelyn is blissfully happy and Max is alone, bitterly regretting his foolishness. Perhaps the best course of action for subjects with the distinctive grilled Mount of Venus is to rule out marriage completely until middle age.

CASE HISTORY
CASE HISTORY

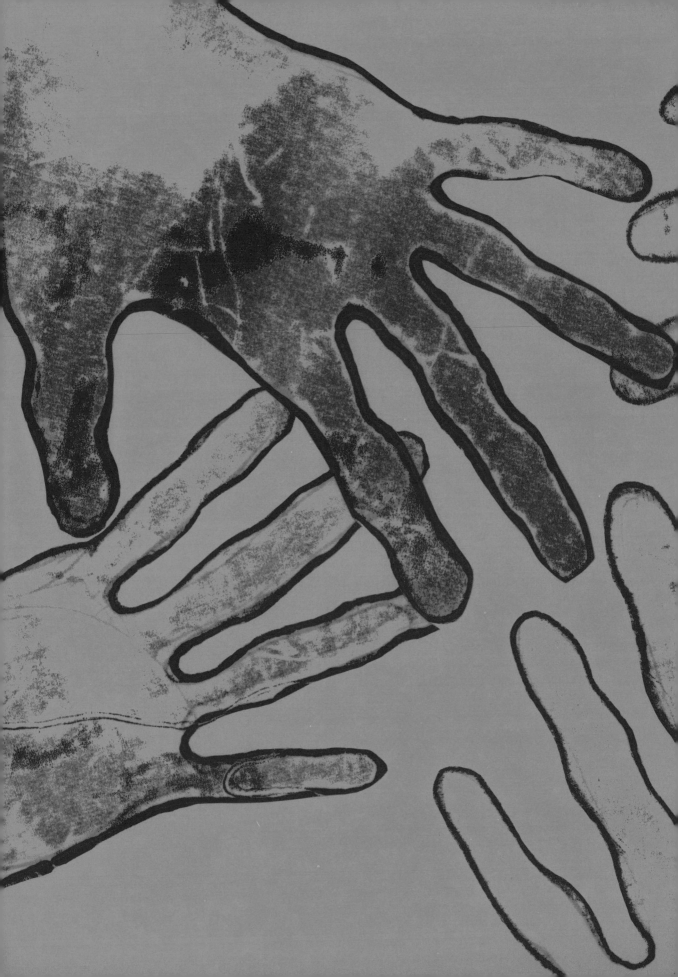

palm
prints

PALM PRINTS

By now, if you have followed all the steps outlined in the previous chapter, you will be able to tell a great deal about your subject without once resorting to what he or she thinks of as "palmistry" - the study of the lines on the palm.
In fact, if you would like to blind your subject with science you can explain that you have used the old art of "cheirognomy". This is the term Victorian palmists used to describe the analysis of the outline of the hand, fingers, thumb and nails.
As you will have seen, cheirognomy allows you to build up an amazingly accurate sketch of the personality before you. But this is only the beginning.

Now you are ready to fill in the all important details, the tiny characteristics that make the individual before you the completely unique person he is. This vital information is to be found by studying the lines on the palm and the minute markings that may be discerned between them. The study of these lines is known as "chirology". Once you add chirology to cheirognomy you will have a portrait of your subject that will take his breath away. Obviously if your sitter is with you and has unlimited time, you can ponder over his palms for as long as you like. But sometimes even the most enthusiastic of friends gets impatient, particularly with a novice. In such cases it's much better to work from palm prints.

This is essential if you wish to read your own palm. A palmist always works from the fingers up towards the wrist. The wrist is the top of the hand; the fingers are the bottom. So when you look at your own palm, you are seeing it upside down from the palmist's point of view. Of course you can turn your hand around, but when you do that it becomes twisted and the lines move out of shape. So the only way to read your own palm accurately is to make a print of it.

It's quite useful to take the prints of other people's hands too, if you are going to be reading their palms more than once. Few people realize that the lines on the palm are not irrevocably fixed. They change subtly as the months pass. The major lines won't swing round, change direction or radically transform themselves. No one can alter his personality that drastically. But smaller branch lines can appear or disappear. New lines can start and a whole host of minor markings suddenly becomes visible as circumstances change. In fact it's very interesting to compare prints that were made six months or a year apart. Sometimes the changes can be astonishing.

The simplest, cleanest way to make a print is to photocopy the hands. Place your hands palm down on the machine and get someone else to press the button. The resulting photocopy should be very detailed, showing every line on the palm.

If you don't have access to a photocopier you can always try an old-fashioned but messy alternative. Wash and dry your hands thoroughly. Take a sheet of clean white paper and a lipstick. Smear the lipstick all over the palm and fingers, then press the palm firmly down on to the paper, taking care not to smudge it. Label both hands with the subject's name and indicate which is the major (writing) hand.

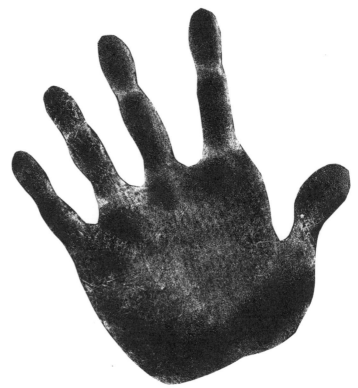

LEFT AND RIGHT HANDS

I've heard it said that the true Romany gypsies concentrate on the left hand only when they read palms because they believe the left hand is closest to the heart. Western tradition is rather different. We consider both hands, but we call them the major and the minor hands. The major hand is the predominant hand, the hand you write with - usually the right hand. The minor hand is the hand you don't write with - usually the left hand.

It's important to study both hands carefully. Generally the left hand shows the potential the subject was born with - his inheritance, if you like. It reveals his basic personality, abilities and any latent talents he might have.

The major hand, which is often more strongly marked shows what the subject has done with his inheritance. Ideally you should see subtle, positive changes which indicate that the subject has fulfilled his potential and made good use of every inborn talent and skill. That is the ideal. Unfortunately not everyone does make good use of their potential. One of the saddest sights I see is a pair of hands in which the minor hand shows some wonderful talent while the major hand shows only laziness and indolence. When this happens I know that the subject has wasted a great gift simply because he couldn't be bothered to pursue it.

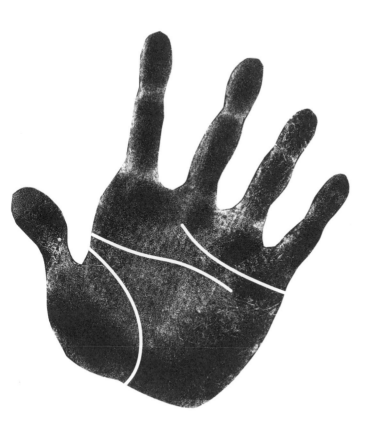

Now you have a fine set of prints, clearly labelled, and you know which is the major hand and which is the minor hand. You are ready to begin studying the lines.

When you look at people's palms you will notice that while some seem to be covered in a network of tiny lines and others seem almost bare, they all have one thing in common. Except for a very few exceptional cases which I'll come back to later, every palm is bisected by three main lines.

No matter how many other lines are present these three dominate the hand quite unmistakably. They are the Life line, which curls around the base of the thumb; the Heart line, which swings across from the outside of the hand beneath the fingers; and between the two of them, the Head line.

These three lines form the basic framework on which the rest of the analysis can be hung. We will look at each line separately.

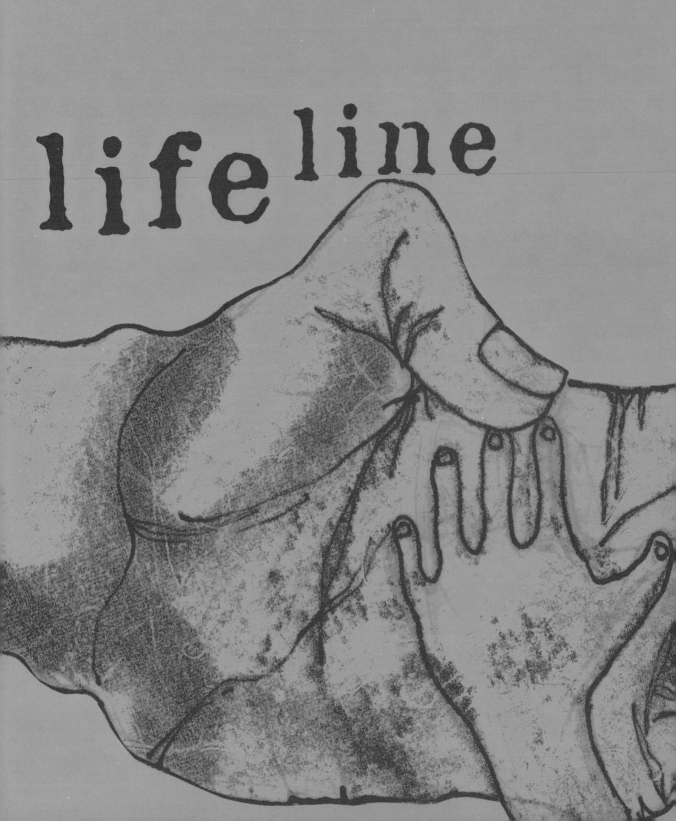

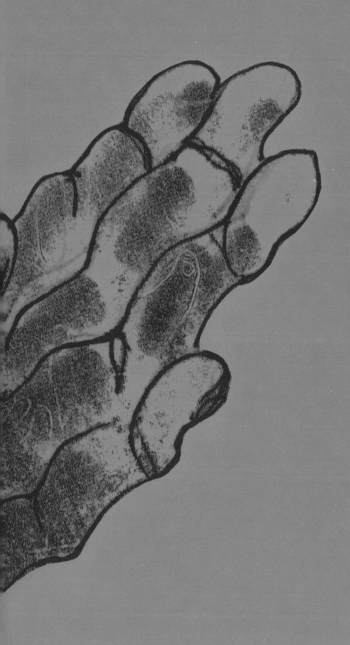

LIFE LINE

The Life line measures vitality

Some time ago a quirky little article appeared in the national press about an experiment conducted by some researchers at a teaching hospital. During their coffee break one day it seems the subject of palmistry came up. Most of the researchers pooh-poohed the idea that there could be any truth in the accuracy of hand-reading but one or two were more open-minded. Surely there must be something in it, they said, or palmistry would have died out years ago. In the end they decided to settle the disagreement with a little test. They all went down to the hospital morgue and asked to see every corpse over seventy years of age. Then they solemnly studied the hands of each elderly ex-patient. To their astonishment they discovered that every one of them had a long Life line.

The sceptics still refused to believe there was any truth in palmistry, but they had to admit it made them think. The open-minded researchers were delighted because they felt this evidence proved their belief in palmistry was justified.

Now when I read that story I couldn't help smiling to myself at their ignorance. While I was pleased that at least they were prepared to discuss the subject of palmistry seriously, I realized that they knew so little about the ancient science that their experiment was worthless. The whole thing was based on a misconception. The researchers thought, as do many people, that the Life line predicts the length of the subject's life. This is quite untrue. The Life line indicates the quality rather than the quantity of life. It measures vitality, energy, the intensity of the life force itself.

energy, the intensity of the life force itself

Those researchers had discovered an interesting coincidence, that's all. By pure chance the elderly hands they studied had belonged to people who were lucky enough to live strong and vigorous lives almost to the end.

Unfortunately this misunderstanding about the meaning of the Life life causes a great deal of anxiety. Within days of the newspaper story appearing I began getting dozens of worried enquiries about the role of the Life line, but one particular letter stood out. The reader was frantic. She was the mother of three young children and she had a short Life line. When she read in the paper that scientists seemed to have proved a connection between a long Life line and a long life, she became convinced that she was destined for an early grave. She enclosed her hand print and asked if I thought she would ever see her children grow up.

I was able to reassure her that there was every indication in her palm that she would live a long and happy life. In her case the brief Life line simply indicated that she ran out of energy at times and should try to pace herself.

Incidentally, no reputable palmist would ever make a prediction of death, no matter what she saw or thought she saw in a hand. This is illegal. Should you ever meet a palmist who claims to make such predictions she is obviously a charlatan and not to be taken seriously.

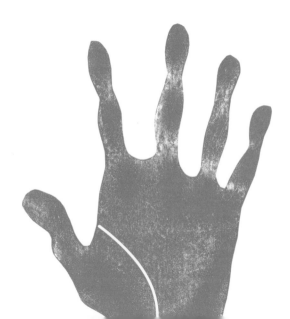

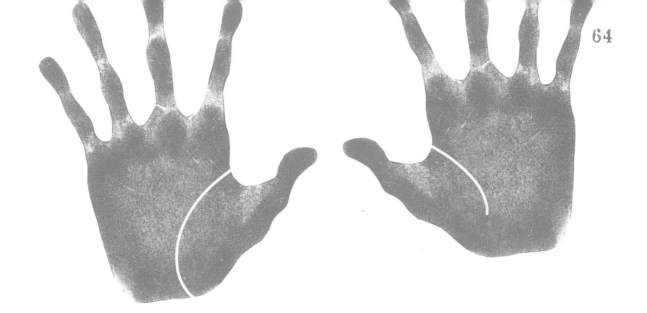

THE LONG LIFE LINE

The ideal Life line is long, clear and boldly marked, starting from the side of the palm beneath the first finger of Jupiter and running smoothly round the Mount of Venus in a great arc. This suggests a robust constitution, good health and abundant energy.

Sometimes the Life line begins in this fashion and then gradually becomes fainter near the wrist. This means that in later life, probably old age, the subject is likely to become more fragile and needs to take greater care of his health.

THE SHORT LIFE LINE

The short Life line, particularly if it is pale, chained and faintly marked, indicates a weaker constitution. These subjects tend to lack energy and don't have as much physical stamina as their friends with stronger Life lines.

They may be prone to frequent colds and various aches and pains. Yet there is no reason why they can't live long and healthy lives. I have even seen cases where subjects with this type of line make a conscious effort to take plenty of rest and improve their diet and months later, the Life line looks stronger and more robust.

MIXED LIFE LINES

It is quite common to find that the Life line in one hand differs from the Life line in the other. When there is a strong Life line in the major hand (usually the right) and a short Life line in the minor hand (usually the left), it indicates

that the subject suffered ill health in childhood but has successfully overcome the early problems. When the minor hand has a strong Life line and the major hand has a weak one, it suggests that something about the subject's pre-

sent lifestyle is sapping his strength and vitality.

The potential for good health is there but for some reason the subject is not willing or able to take advantage of it.

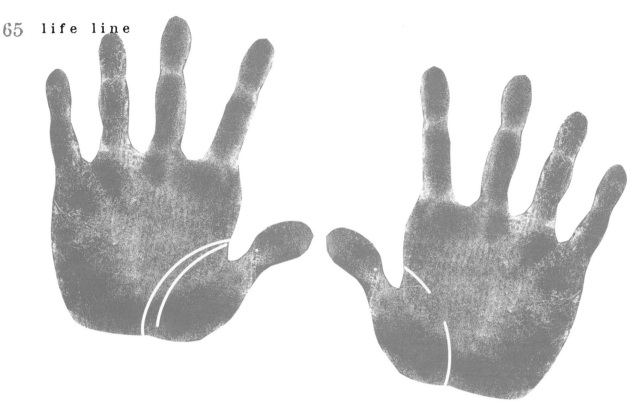

DOUBLE LIFE LINE

double life line
double life line

Occasionally another fainter line can be seen behind the Life line, mirroring the Life line's course like a pale ghost. This is known as a double Life line and it is a very fortunate sign. The subject with a double Life line walks through life with a guardian angel. No matter what illnesses or accidents he meets with, he will always bounce back good as new.

A BREAK IN THE LIFE LINE

It is quite common for a Life line to have a break in it at some point. This is no cause for alarm. It does not mean that the subject is about to die, simply that they are likely to suffer an illness or accident, probably of a minor nature. Look closely and you will usually see a tiny line behind the break. This is a repair line. Once the subject is completely recovered the break in the Life line will probably disappear from the hand and the repair line will fade away.

Sometimes the repair line is crossed by another line that leads through the break and out towards the palm. In this case it suggests that the subject is about to begin a new life, completely different from that which went before. It may mean a new marriage or a powerful relationship, or simply a new career or the relocation of a job to another part of the country. Whatever the cause, this mark suggests a break with the past and a fresh start. It is a positive sign.

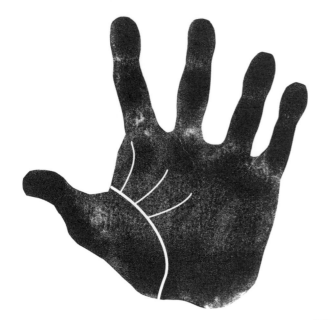

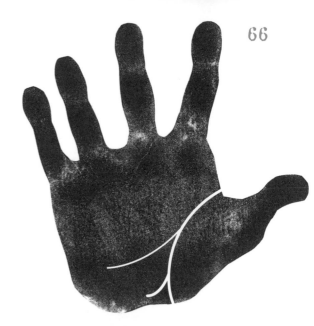

UPWARD BRANCHING LINES

Generally speaking, lines that spring up from the Life line towards the fingers are welcome signs. They show success, advancement and gains both material and emotional. To determine in which area the improvement is likely to be found you need to check the direction of the line.

Lines pointing towards the first finger of Jupiter suggest promotion and enhanced status.

Lines pointing towards the second finger of Saturn indicate success achieved possibly at the expense of others.

Lines pointing towards the third finger of Apollo are particularly exciting, because they suggest good luck and possibly even fame. I would expect a lottery winner or someone who receives a sudden windfall to have such a line.

Lines pointing towards the fourth finger of Mercury show some sort of gain achieved through good communication. Perhaps the subject is a salesman, politician, media worker or teacher. Or possibly he has landed himself a new job through a particularly successful interview.

DOWNWARD BRANCHING LINES

Downward branching lines usually speak of disappointments. However, when the lines sweep down and out towards the Mount of the Moon on the opposite edge of the palm, they have a different meaning altogether. This type of marking suggests a powerful urge to travel. When it is accompanied by a Life line that ends in a fork, one prong angled towards the base of the thumb and the other towards the Mount of the Moon, it indicates that the subject may emigrate.

Occasionally a downward branching line will swing off the Life line and come to rest on the Success line, connecting the two in the centre of the palm. This shows that the subject is likely to travel abroad as part of her job. It could also suggest inheriting property overseas.

CASE HISTORY
SHORT LIFE LINE
- LONG LIFE

The oldest person I've ever met was a vivacious lady of 103. Confined to hospital by this time she was nevertheless bright, cheerful and interested in everything that was going on around her. She sat in a chair in the dayroom with a neat little crochet bonnet on her head tied under her chin with a ribbon, and she regaled her visitors with memories of the old days when she could buy a loaf of bread for a farthing.

Fascinated, I studied her hands for any clues relating to her great longevity. Both were long and soft. On the left hand, her minor hand, the Life line was long and strong, but on the right hand, her major hand, the Life line stopped short.

This showed that while she had a great zest for life, she also lacked stamina and could tire easily. Provided she took rest whenever she felt really exhausted she would be fine - as indeed she had proved to be, managing to outlive all her "long Life-lined" contemporaries.

Interestingly, the clues that pointed to her extraordinarily long life were found not in her Life line but in her Head and Heart lines. The old lady had a very deeply marked, strong Head line showing her keen awareness and intellect despite her great age and she also had a double Heart line, which is very unusual.

CASE HISTORY
CASE HISTORY

CASE HISTORY

heart line

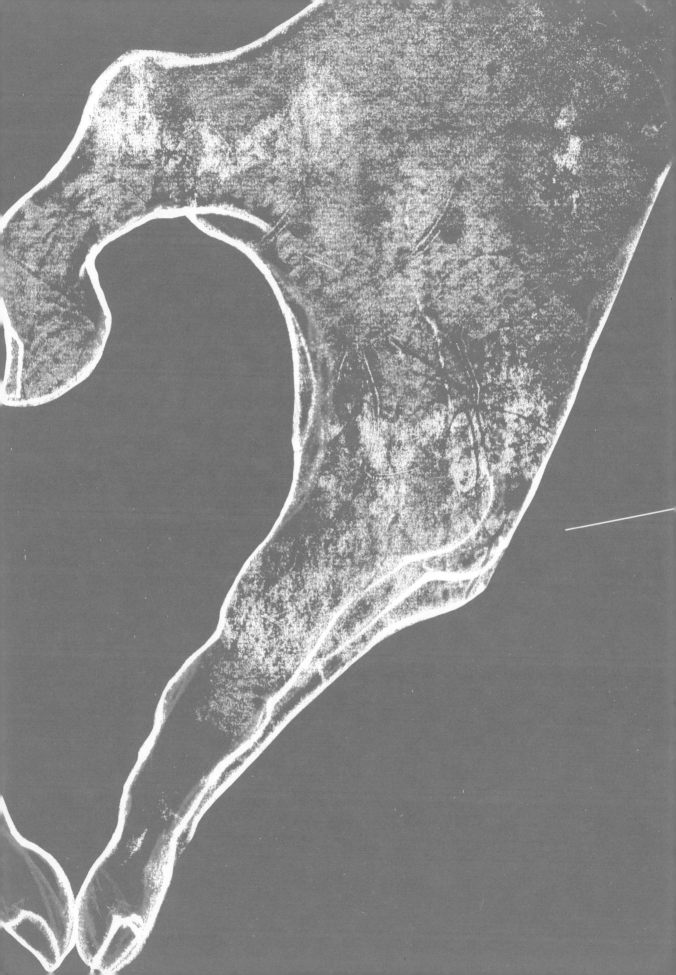

The Heart line reveals the strength of th

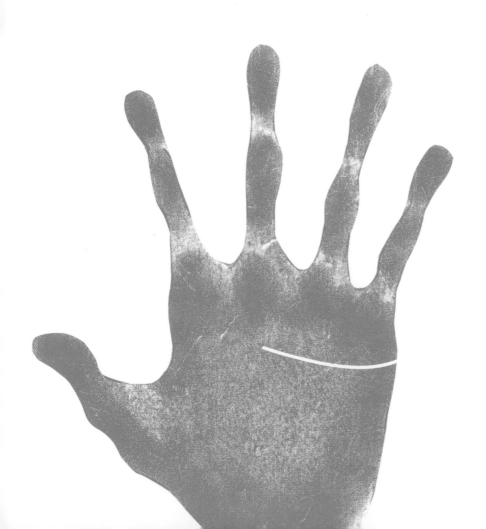

HEART LINE

The Heart line is the first major line of the hand, as it is found right at the top of the palm, just below the base of the fingers. It starts at the outside edge of the palm and moves across in the general direction of the thumb. Although the Life line is better known, the Heart line is often of more interest because, as its name suggests, it deals with matters of the heart, both literally and metaphorically.

emotions and the individual's potential for love.

It can indicate whether a relationship is running smoothly or heading for the rocks. It can show whether the subject is loyal and true or a fickle flirt. But it can also give many clues to the person's health and physical stamina. Palmists of old believed that the Heart line was linked directly to the heart itself. While we recognize today that this may not be literally true, it is amazing what the Heart line can reveal about conditions that could well affect the chest. A delicate Heart line suggests a nervous disposition. The individual with this type of line finds stress and strain particularly hard to bear and should try to lead as calm a life as possible. Yoga and gentle exercise are especially beneficial in these cases and high pressure careers are best avoided.

There are several important aspects to check when studying the Heart line: position, shape, colour and length must all be taken into account before looking at the various smaller lines that often spring from it. The shape and length of the Heart line can vary tremendously. Some move across the hand straight as an arrow while others swing in a wide curve as pronounced as the Life line. Some are very short, barely reaching the base of the third finger of Apollo. Others stretch right across the hand, finally coming to rest under the first finger of Jupiter.

The final resting place of the Heart line is particularly signficant. In some people the Heart line is one simple line from start to finish. In others, it breaks up into two or more branches at the end. I've seen Heart lines terminate in branches that look like tiny fans.

Generally speaking, the simpler the Heart line, the less complicated the love life. When the Heart line fragments into two or more branches it suggests complex emotions and a need for variety in relationships.

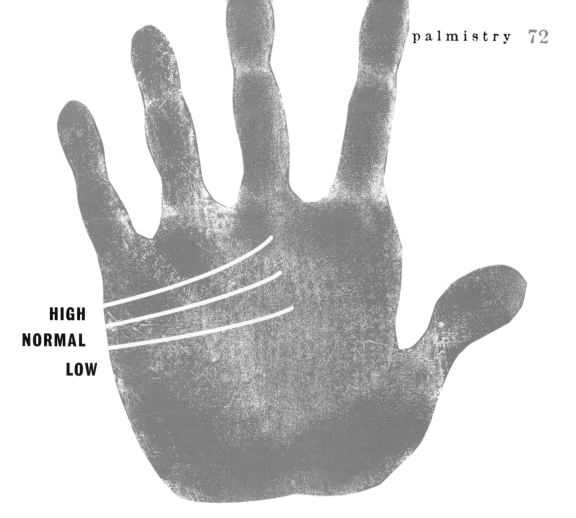

HIGH

NORMAL

LOW

HIGH-SET HEART LINE

When the Heart line is set very high in the hand, close to the base of the fingers, it suggests a wildly impulsive, dramatic character who frequently falls in and out of love. This is the type who will fly his beloved to Paris the day after meeting her, but three weeks later he might have forgotten her name.

LOW-SET HEART LINE

When the Heart line is set low in the hand, almost half way down the palm, the opposite applies. Here is a character who is ultra cautious in matters of the heart. He is extremely wary about falling in love and it takes a long time to win his affections.

NORMAL-SET HEART LINE

The normal Heart line is midway between these two extreme positions. It has a neat, well balanced appearance in the palm and indicates a sensible individual with a healthy approach to love. She isn't rash with her affections but neither is she afraid of being hurt.

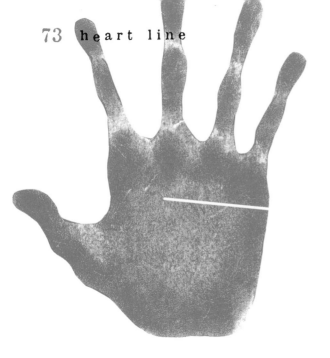 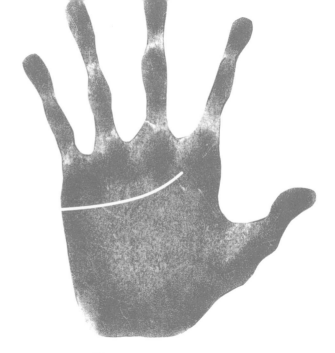

STRAIGHT HEART LINE

When the Heart line is straight it indicates a matter-of-fact, rather unemotional nature. Subjects with this type of Heart line are unlikely to be found writing sonnets and dreaming up romantic evenings for two. They may feel love quite deeply, but they are not demonstrative.

CURVED HEART LINE

When the Heart line is curved as a bowstring it denotes an emotional, sentimental character. The more rounded the curve, the closer to the surface the emotions are likely to be. These types really do wear their hearts on their sleeves.

PINK HEART LINE

The ideal colour for the Heart line is a clear, well-defined pink. This indicates a person who is well-balanced sexually and emotionally.

RED HEART LINE

A red Heart line suggests a deeply passionate nature - this type of line belongs to the subject who is more interested in the sexual side of a relationship than the emotional.

Should the line deepen almost to purple in colour, it indicates that love and violence are closely linked in the subject's mind.

PALE HEART LINE

When the Heart line is so pale as to be almost colourless it suggests a lack of stamina and vigour. These subjects long for love but have little interest in sex. They prefer a meeting of minds in relationships.

HEART LINE REACHING APOLLO

When the Heart line comes only to the third finger of Apollo it indicates a person who is not particularly interested in relationships. Love and other such sentimental notions mean little to him. He may even feel genuinely puzzled as to what everyone else is going on about. Romance, he believes, is greatly overrated. He may well enjoy casual affairs, but he doesn't ever want to get involved.

HEART LINE REACHING SATURN

When the Heart line terminates beneath the second finger of Saturn it suggests a lover who is inclined to be rather selfish in bed. These types are more interested in their own physical gratification than in building relationships. They let their partner make any compromises or sacrifices necessary to keep things going.

Should the line reach Saturn and then turn suddenly down towards the Head line, it shows an individual whose head rules his heart. These types would never choose an unsuitable partner and wouldn't hesitate in terminating a relationship if it ceased to please them.

If the Heart line reaches Saturn and then suddenly turns up to come to rest between the fingers of Saturn and Jupiter, it suggests a jealous, possessive streak.

HEART LINE REACHING JUPITER

When the Heart line comes to rest beneath the base of the first finger of Jupiter it suggests an affectionate, loyal and trusting nature. If the line divides into two at the end it shows that the subject is an idealist in matters of the heart and can sometimes act rashly.

If the line turns up towards the finger it shows that the subject likes to put her beloved on a pedestal. Should the Heart line actually start to climb the finger, a rare sign, it reveals an individual who carries adoration far too far. Admiration can turn to fanatical hero-worship.

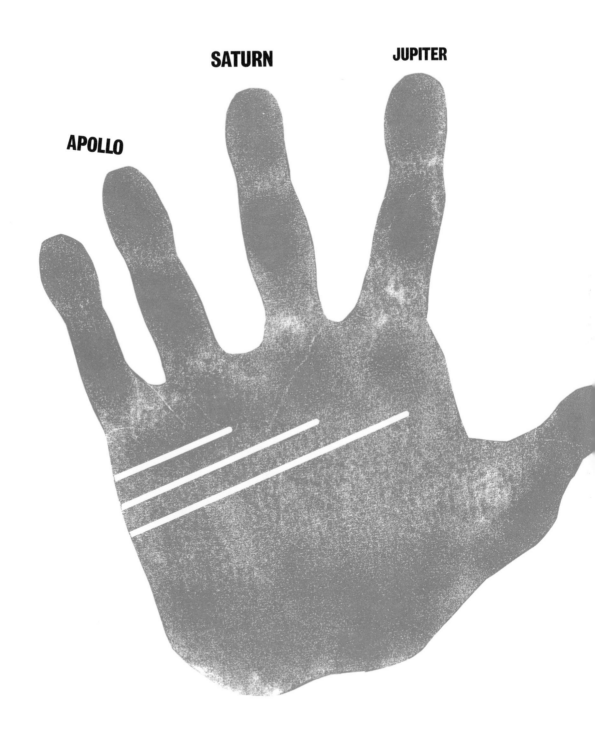

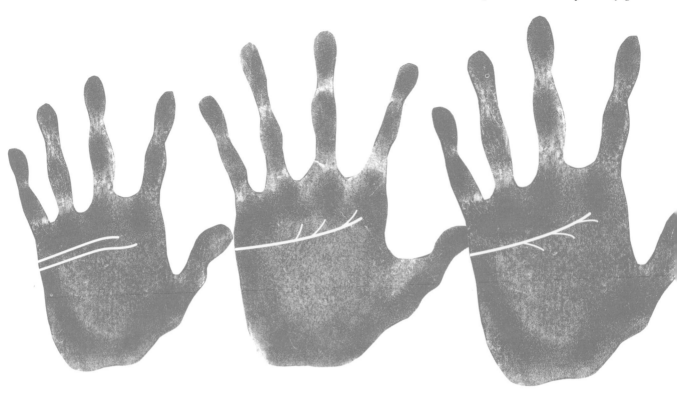

DOUBLE HEART LINE

double heart line
double heart line

As I mentioned earlier, I saw a double Heart line in the hand of an old lady of 103. This is a very fortunate sign. It indicates robust health, a particularly strong heart and the physical and emotional vigour to withstand the stresses and strains of life.

UPWARD BRANCHING LINES

When lines sweep up off the Heart line towards the fingers it is very good news. They suggest happy, positive relationships, partners in harmony with each other.

DOWNWARD BRANCHING LINES

These are not a welcome sight. Downward branching lines indicate disappointments in love and difficult patches in a relationship. Other areas of life could well start going wrong too. Fortunately if the line continues smoothly after the branch it suggests that everything will settle down again.

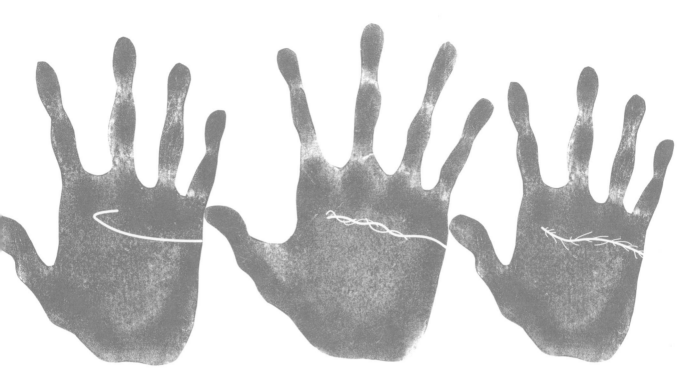

BACKWARD CURVING LINES

It is unusual to see the Heart line turn back on itself, but occasionally this does happen. I have seen the Heart line progress normally across the palm and then suddenly twist back in the opposite direction so that it is pointing towards the fourth finger of Mercury. This shows a mercenary attitude towards love and relationships. It might be quite unconscious, but the subject is likely to be drawn romantically to partners who are wealthy. I have seen this type of Heart line in the hands of young women who marry rich, older men.

CHAINED LINES

The chained Heart line is quite unmistakable. Instead of running solidly across the hand, it appears to be made up of interlocking rings, like links in a chain. This convoluted structure reflects the subject's emotions, which are complicated and changeable. The lover with this type of Heart line cannot commit himself to one partner and is unlikely to be faithful for very long.

FEATHERED LINES

Sometimes there are so many lines rising and falling from the Heart line that it has a feather-like appearance. This does not indicate a roller-coaster love life packed with good and bad experiences. Rather, it suggests that the subject is an incorrigible flirt. There may well be a great many good and bad romantic episodes, but these will come about because the subject can't help testing out her attractiveness on every possible occasion.

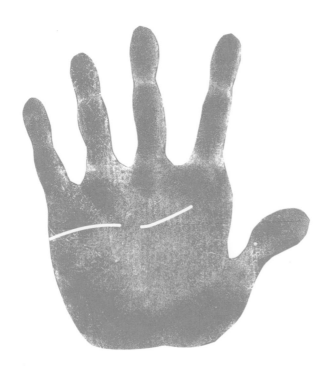

BROKEN HEART LINE

A complete break in the Heart line can be an alarming sight if it is not properly understood. It suggests an emotional drama of some kind. Often there is a crisis in a relationship at this time or even a bout of ill health. However, often a faint sister-line appears around the break to heal the hurt, but even if it doesn't, at the other side of the break the Heart line continues smoothly on its way.

This suggests that the problem will be overcome and the subject will get back on an even keel.

CASE HISTORY

THE JEALOUS HEART LINE

When Anna came to see me she was wearing the most beautiful emerald and diamond engagement ring. But when I admired it, tears came into her eyes.

Her pride in the lovely ring had turned to sorrow. Now it seemed to symbolize everything that was wrong in her life. Apparently she and her fiancé Chris had been engaged for eight months, but now he was talking about calling off the wedding. He had become cool and distant and Anna couldn't understand what was wrong. She feared he had fallen for someone else.

Yet when I looked at her palm I began to wonder if the problem lay with Anna herself and not with Chris at all. Her Heart line swept across her hand and came to rest high up between the fingers of Saturn and Jupiter. It was the classic jealous Heart line.

Tactfully I asked if Anna tended to be a little possessive. Suddenly the whole story came out. Chris had always been loyal to her but he was such a goodlooking man that Anna couldn't stop worrying that one day he would go off with someone else.

She flew into a temper if he even glanced at another girl and insisted that he spent every spare moment in her company so that temptation couldn't come his way. No wonder the poor man was having doubts about the marriage. He wanted a wife, not a jailor.

I asked to see prints of Chris's hands and I was able to reassure Anna that he was a loyal, loving man. She had nothing to fear, but she must curb her jealous streak, as it was ruining their relationship.

Anna did indeed work hard to suppress her fears and to give Chris more freedom. After a while she discovered that she felt happier than ever before. It hadn't been any fun watching her fiancé like a policeman every moment of the day. Now she was more relaxed and able to enjoy herself. In fact occasionally other men were chatting her up, making Chris a little jealous.

Six months later I received a piece of wedding cake in a little silver box. The wedding had gone ahead and the last I heard was that Anna and Chris were very happy.

CASE HISTORY
CASE HISTORY

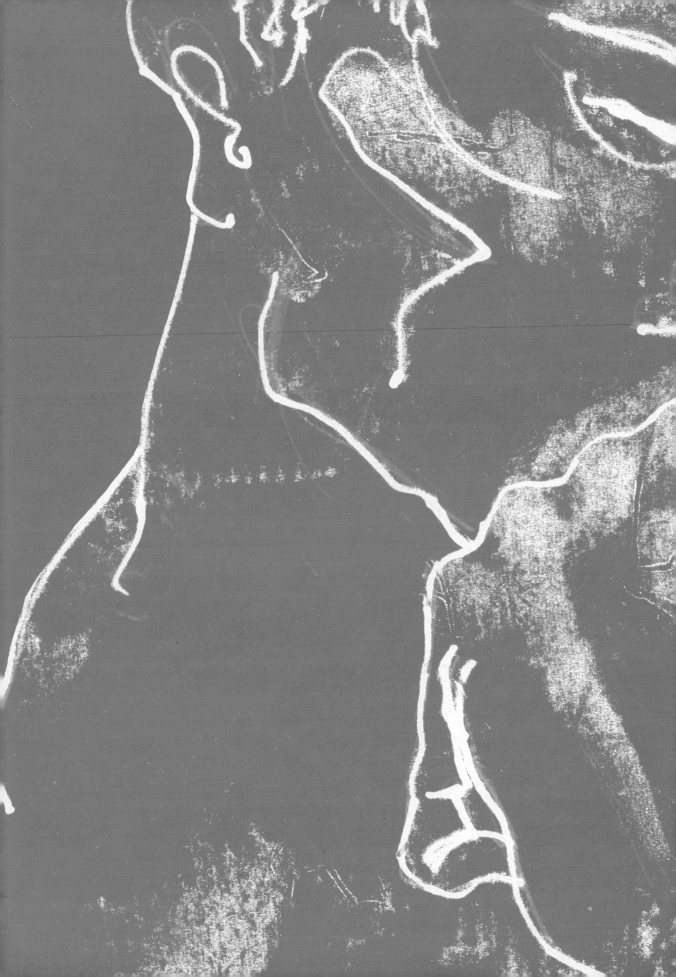

head line

HEAD LINE
The Head line gives valuable insight

The last of the major lines of the hand is the Head line. This is found between the Heart line and the Life line at the side of the palm. It starts beneath the first finger of Jupiter and begins to journey across the hand in the opposite direction to the Heart line.

Just as the Heart line is concerned with the emotions and matters of the heart, the Head line deals with the intellect, the powers of concentration and the individual's approach to problems. The Head line shows whether the subject tends to react to challenges with logical analysis or whether she adopts an imaginative, intuitive approach.

The Head line, when considered together with the qualities of the thumb, gives valuable insight into the type of career to which the subject might be suited. It gives clues as to academic ability and shows whether the invidual is likely to have to a good memory or not. It can even gauge the level of confidence and independence present. There are several details that must be considered when studying the Head line. Length, position in the hand, colour and course should all be noted with care.

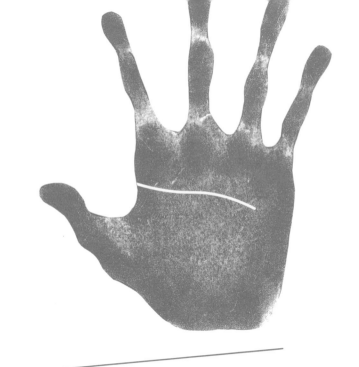

nto career and intellectual ability

Generally speaking, the longer the Head line the greater the intelligence. The length varies greatly. Some Head lines reach only to the second finger of Saturn, while others stretch almost right across the palm. However, it must be remembered that intelligence alone is no guarantee of success in life. Other factors such as confidence, a likeable personality, determination, persistence and energy are all equally important.

I have seen individuals with comparatively short Head lines who went on to be immensely successful, and I have seen subjects with very long Head lines who were unable to put their intelligence to good use because they lacked the other vital qualities.

The shape of the Head line is not uniform in every hand. Some are straight as rulers, others tilt gently, and some swing towards the wrist in a distinct curve. Each of these variations has its own meaning.

SHORT HEAD LINE

When the Head line reaches only to the second finger of Saturn it suggests poor concentration and difficulty with analytical thought. These subjects would be wise to avoid academic pursuits - they probably loathe book work anyway - and they should concentrate on developing their other talents and skills.

HEAD LINE REACHING APOLLO

This is a medium length Head line denoting a good brain, a person in whom commonsense and the power of abstract thought are well balanced. These types are unlikely to become professors or rocket scientists but they have the intellect to choose from a wide variety of less specialized careers.

HEAD LINE REACHING MERCURY

These are the superbrains of the world. Subjects with very long Head lines have extremely good memories and the ability to concentrate singlemindedly on one subject until they have learned all there is to know. They are capable of highly academic or scientific careers, but they may choose to follow a quite unexpected course. I believe the singer Madonna has a very long Head line. She has obviously used her intelligence to mastermind her musical career and keep track of her finances.

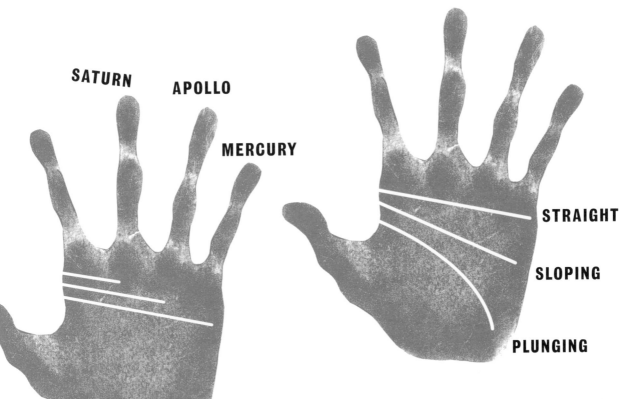

SATURN

APOLLO

MERCURY

STRAIGHT

SLOPING

PLUNGING

STRAIGHT HEAD LINE

When the Head line marches across the palm like a soldier it suggests a subject whose head rules his heart. Shrewd and businesslike, he is often good at handling financial matters, but his love life tends to suffer. This is an individual who will always put work before pleasure. They are often very successful in their careers but home life can be quite a different story.

SLOPING HEAD LINE

Often the Head line starts high up under the first finger of Jupiter and then slopes gently down to the centre of the palm. This is the sign of an active imagination and linked to a curve at the side of the palm suggests an artistic gift. Should the curve slope steeply it shows that the subject is inclined to be a dreamer. She must make an effort to put some of those dreams into operation or her life will slip by without achievement.

PLUNGING HEAD LINE

Occasionally the Head line doesn't so much slope as plummet towards the wrist. This is not such a welcome sight as it suggests a tendency towards depression, and in extreme cases, suicidal thoughts. These subjects should recognize that if they feel unusually down they should not try to battle depression on their own, they should seek help.

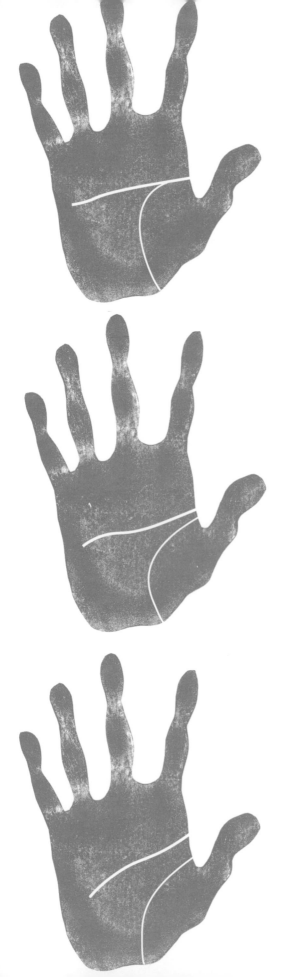

HEAD LINE COMBINED WITH LIFE LINE

Many Head lines begin on the edge of the palm, tightly linked to the Life line. This shows close family ties in the early years. When the two lines continue together for some distance it indicates a lack of confidence and little need for independence.

SEPARATE HEAD LINE

When the Head line is self-contained, starting close to the Life line but not touching it, it indicates a confident, independent character who likes to make her own decisions.

HEAD LINE STANDING ALONE

Occasionally the Head line stands conspicuously apart from the Life line, leaving a wide gap between the two. This suggests a person so independent that she resents the intrusion of others. She is unlikely to be close to her family and probably has diffi-culty forming genuine friendships.

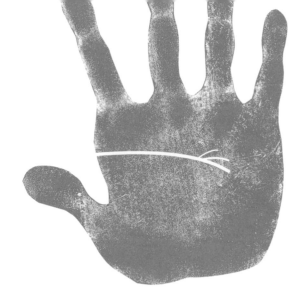

PALE HEAD LINE

A thin, almost white Head line shows a subject who tires easily. These types may be extremely clever but they should pace themselves and not try to tackle too much at a time. Students in particular with this type of Head line should take care to study little and often and avoid last minute cramming for examinations.

FORKED HEAD LINE

Most Head lines run their course as a clear, single line but sometimes right at the end they split into a pronounced fork. This is known as the "writer's fork" and shows a natural talent for the written word.

RED HEAD LINE

A bold red Head line suggests high energy, great stamina and the ability to get through enormous amounts of work. It could also denote impatience with others less able to cope with so much.

double head line
double head line
DOUBLE HEAD LINE

Like the Life line and the Heart line, the Head line can also be mirrored by another indentical line running parallel to it. This is known as the double Head line and is a very fortunate sign. It shows great cleverness and wonderful powers of concentration. People with double Head lines are never lost for ideas.

PINK HEAD LINE

The ideal Head line is pink and clearly marked, showing a well-balanced, stable approach to mental pursuits.

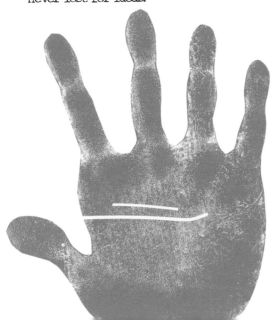

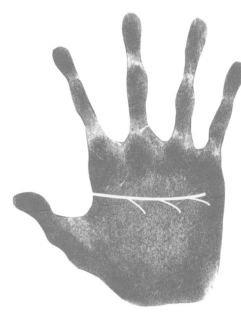

DOWNWARD BRANCHING LINES

Lines that branch downwards from the Head line suggest disappointments that leave the subject feeling melancholy.

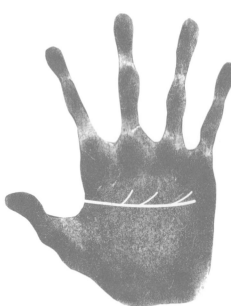

UPWARD BRANCHING LINES

These are fortunate signs showing good news in any matters that require brainpower. They might indicate exam success, a mental task successfuly completed, or a piece of research reaching a satisfactory conclusion. Whatever his field, the subject is likely to receive an intellectual boost of some kind.

CASE HISTORY

THE DEPENDENT SON

CASE HISTORY

Tom was 26 when he came to see me. He was very depressed because his mother had recently died and he was finding it very difficult to come to terms with his loss.

When I looked at his Head line I noticed that it was tightly joined to the Life line for quite a long distance, showing that Tom lacked confidence and was very dependent on his family. Yet his Head line was very long, reaching right across the palm as far as the fourth finger of Mercury. This indicated that Tom possessed a great deal of natural intelligence. The problem was that so far, he had been unable to use it because he was so dependent on his mother.

Apparently Tom's father had abandoned them when the boy was very small and Tom and his mother had become very close. To her, Tom remained a little boy, even when he was obviously grown-up, and she did everything for him. At the age of 26 he had never so much as bought a pair of socks for himself or made his own bed. He had no idea how to cook a meal or pay a bill, and when his mother suddenly died it was a catastrophe for him.

Yet when Tom's Head line parted company with his Life line, both proceeded quite efficiently on their separate paths.

I could see that Tom had the intelligence to master all the tasks so far undertaken by his mother and he would soon learn to appreciate his new independence.

Sure enough, a few months later I met Tom in the supermarket. He was a changed man. He strode confidently around with an eager sparkle in his eye and he was quite clearly enjoying being in charge of his own life for the first time.

CASE HISTORY

CASE HIST

success
line

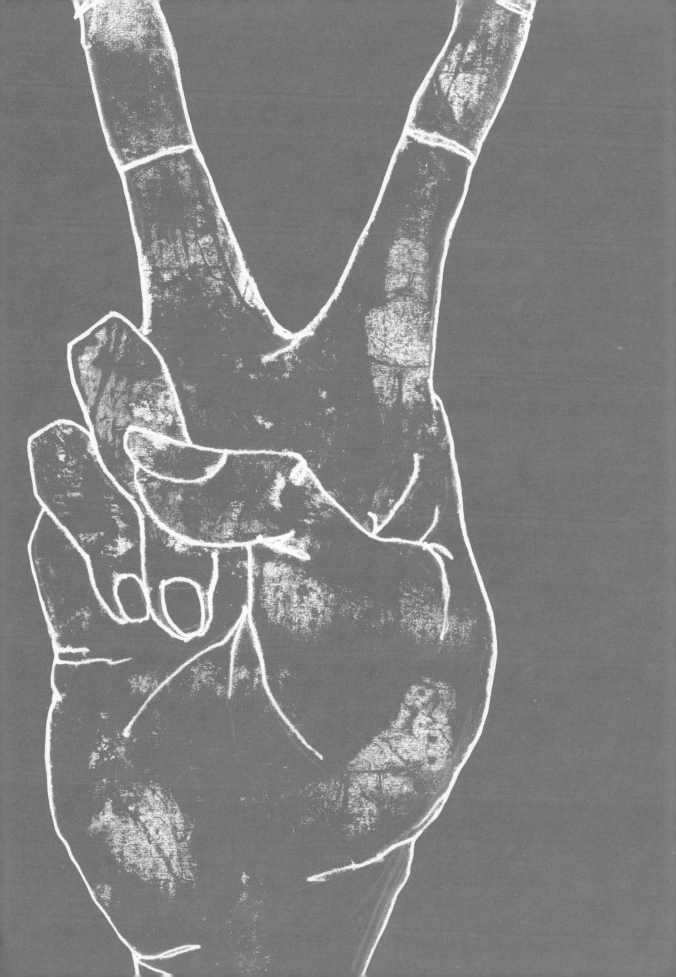

SUCCESS LINE

Once you have learned all you can about the major lines, you will notice that many hands have other well-defined lines. These are the minor lines. This does not mean that they are of little account, in fact they often contain important information, but they do not represent the crucial matters dealt with by the major lines: the life force, the emotions and the intellect.
All the lines of the hand are subject to changes now and again, but the minor lines change most of all. They can fade away if circumstances alter, or they can suddenly appear and grow if something new enters the picture.

This is a tantalizing line

Perhaps the most interesting of all these lines is the Success line. This is a tantalizing line because some people do not possess it at all, while others have a such a bold, strong marking that it appears to dominate their whole palm. As its name suggests, this line deals with the potential for worldly success, a fulfilling career and ambitions achieved. The complete absence of a Success line does not mean that the subject is a miserable failure at everything she undertakes. It simply suggests that worldly matters are of little interest. Material gain and burning ambitions come very low down on this individual's list of priorities. I have never seen the hands of Mother Theresa, but I would not be surprised to learn that - successful as the rest of the world believes her to be - she lacks a Success line.

The Success line always runs vertically up the palm, but it does not follow a set course as do the Life line, Heart line and Head lines. It can start from a number of different places. It can be one straight track or it can be made up of several lines, loosely connected.

Sometimes there is a series of lines, branching and weaving and changing direction all over the palm, yet always ascending towards the fingers. This type of marking suggests an individual who frequently changes jobs or even switches career midstream as he climbs to the top.

In some hands, the Success line starts strongly and then comes to a complete halt at the Head line or the Heart line. When it stops at the Head line, this means that the subject's ambitions have had to be put on hold through circumstances beyond his control. When the Success line stops at the Heart line, it shows that a relationship has blocked the individual's career in some way.

because some people do not possess it at all

Often realizing the cause of the problem is enough to get the subject back on the right track. When this happens, the Success line tends to start again above the line that was blocking it.

In some hands the Success line fades, only to strengthen again, suggesting career difficulties that are eventually overcome. A complete break in the Success line doesn't necessarily foretell disaster. It may indicate a setback that brings ambitions to a halt for a while. Once prospects improve, the Success line will continue on its way.

One frequently observed sign is a whole series of small Success line offshoots on the Mount of Apollo. This is a warning that the subject has too many irons in the fire. He may well have felt it was a good idea to diversify, but these lines show he is spreading his talents too thinly and will achieve nothing.

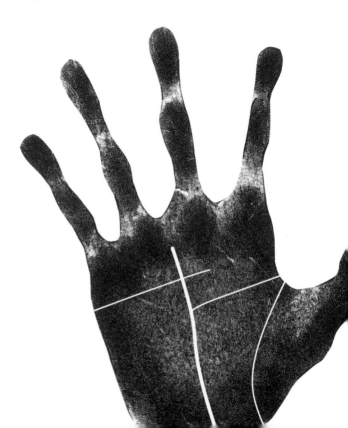

SIMPLE SUCCESS LINE

The simplest Success line starts at the base of the hand and runs up to the fingers in a straight line.

This type of line belongs to the individual who has always known what he wanted to do, who has set himself a goal and gone for it single-mindedly. These people often have a sense of destiny. They are not sure where they will end up, but they know instinctively that there is something they must do.

The straightforward Success line is always a good sign. The finger under which the line comes to rest tells more about the kind of success that will be achieved.

success

success

DOUBLE SUCCESS LINE

This is an unusual and very promising sign. When the Success line has a similar line running parallel to it, it suggests that the subject is destined for great success in two separate fields.

SUCCESS LINE BEGINNING HIGH IN THE HAND

When the Success line does not begin in the usual place, at the base of the hand near the wrist, but high in the hand, it shows that goals were not easily achieved in early life. Sometimes the subject could not decide on the right career, or perhaps she was too preoccupied with relationships and family to think about her ambitions. It could also be that luck was simply not on her side and so every venture failed.

Whatever the reason, this type of Success line indicates a late starter. The right path will be discovered in later years, and then the individual will forge ahead.

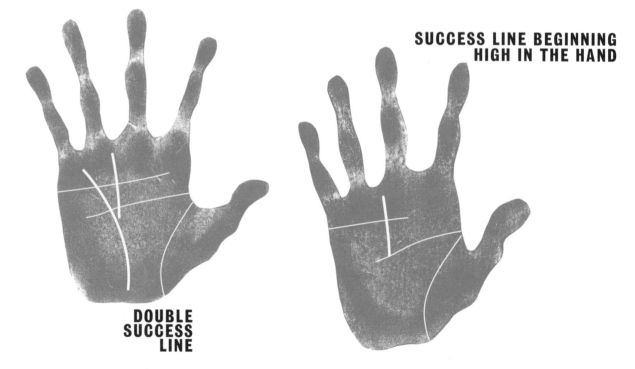

SUCCESS LINE BEGINNING HIGH IN THE HAND

DOUBLE SUCCESS LINE

MERCURY SUCCESS LINE

When the Success line goes up to the fourth finger of Mercury and that finger is long, the likelihood is that the subject will achieve success through wheeling and dealing. These types love the politics of persuading others to accept their point of view. Although they are successful, they have no wish to sit back and enjoy the fruits of their labours. It is the excitement of the work itself that attracts them, and no matter how wealthy they become, they have no wish to retire.

APOLLO SUCCESS LINE

If you could choose, this is the Success line to have. Everything comes easily to the subject with this type of line. He seems to have the golden touch. Every venture works out well, every tiny setback turns out to be a blessing in disguise. He walks a magic path straight to his goals. If there is a star on the mount next to the line it promises quite spectacular gains.

SATURN SUCCESS LINE

Saturn is a hard taskmaster and lines that end on this mount usually indicate a challenge of some kind. The subject will have to work very hard and overcome a number of obstacles before he achieves his aims. Success is assured, and the subject will certainly have earned it.

JUPITER SUCCESS LINE

Great success, enhanced status and the respect of his peers is likely for the subject with this type of Success line. Should there be a star on the Mount of Jupiter next to it, it is likely that the individual will receive an honour for his achievements.

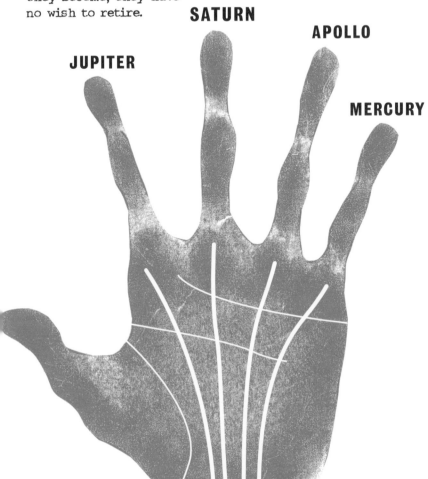

JUPITER

SATURN

APOLLO

MERCURY

other

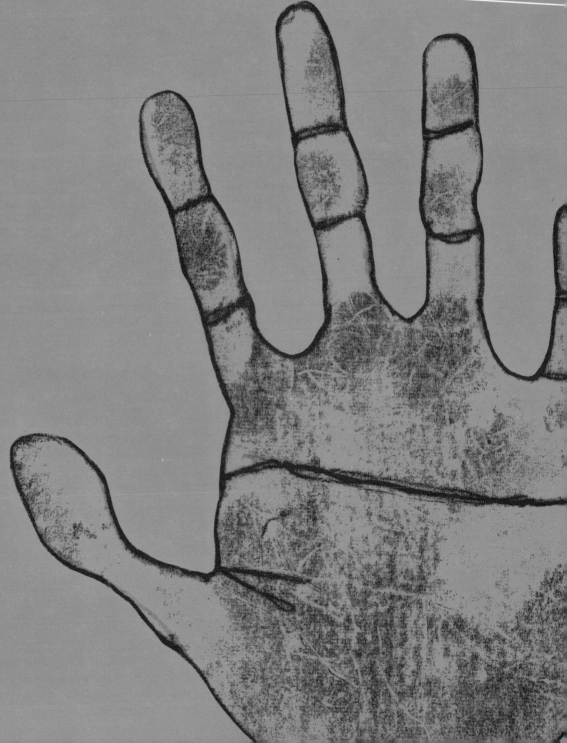

lines

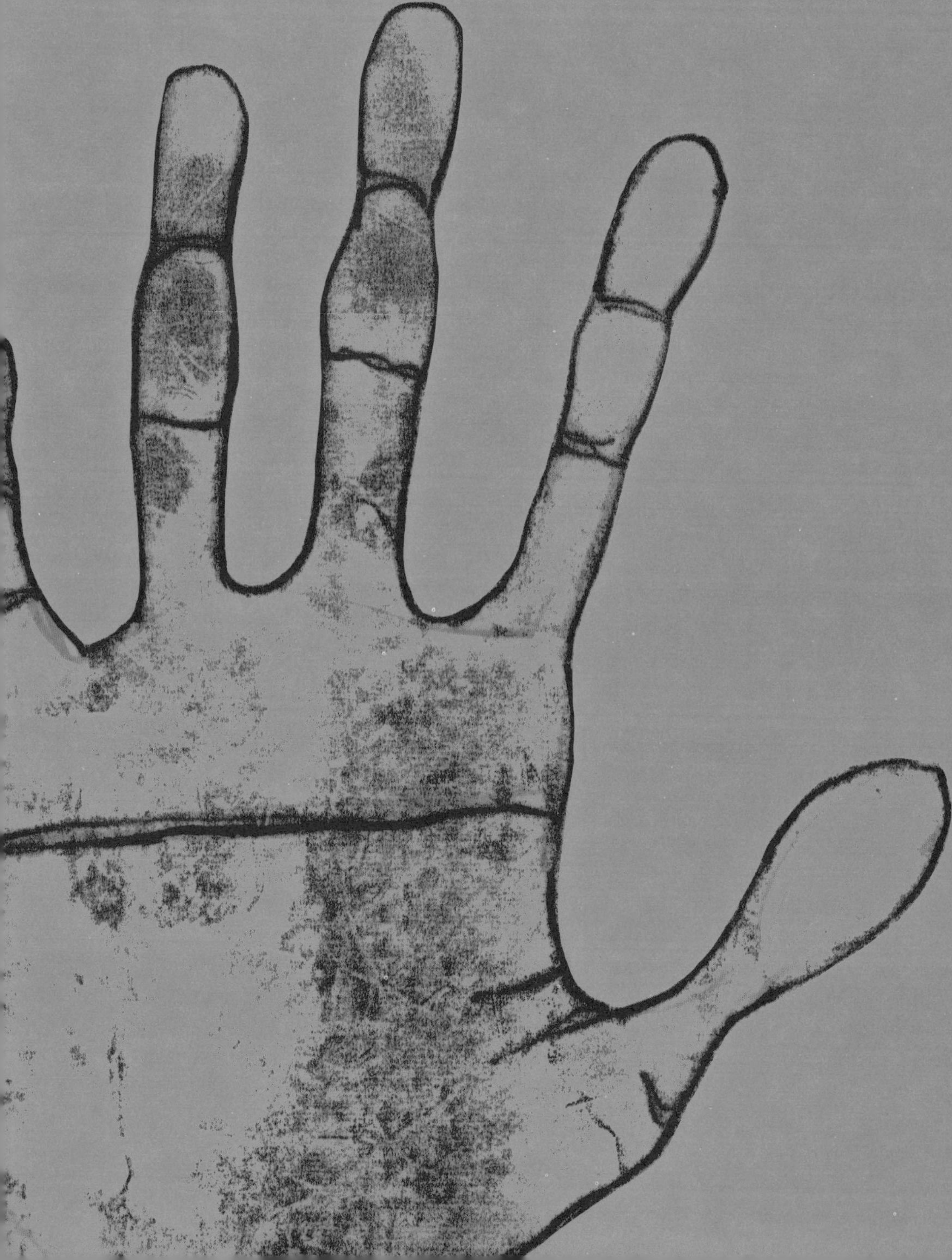

OTHER LINES
AND MARKINGS

In addition to the Success line, there are other lines and markings to look out for on the palm that you are studying. In this chapter I want to tell you about the Simian line, which is often confused with Downs syndrome markings. I also want to discuss the Quadrangle, the area of the hand between the Heart and Head lines. What you find there will give you further insights into your subject's character and his path through life. Finally, I'll introduce you to a selection of minor lines that indicate travel, influence, psychic leanings and the advent of a newcomer in the subject's life.

THE SIMIAN LINE

At the beginning of the book I described the typical Downs syndrome hand recognized by doctors. It is short and broad, with two and not three major lines. The Head and Heart lines are joined to form one uncertain line in the centre of the hand.

However, there is another type of hand in which only two major lines are present. The second line, which replaces the Heart and Head lines, could easily be misinterpreted by the layman as the Downs syndrome line. In fact it is the Simian line.

In this case, the hand is quite normal, except for the fact that there are only two major lines in the palm instead of three. The Life line is as you would expect it to be, but the Head and Heart lines appear to have joined forces and merged into a single dominating line that slashes right across the palm from one side to the other.

When this line, the Simian line, crosses the palm close to the point where the Head line would normally be found, it indicates that the subject is extremely clever - possibly even brilliant. He or she is endowed with some special gift that must be discovered and put to use.

Unfortunately, the bearers of this type of line tend to lack faith in themselves. These types frequently feel unfairly criticized and then upset others by becoming over-defensive. Once they overcome their basic lack of confidence and realize they genuinely have something special to offer, they can transform their lives.

If the Simian line crosses the palm at the point where the Heart line is normally found, the subject is probably very clever, but also selfish and suspicious.

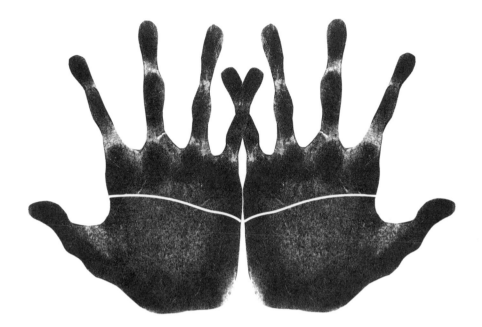

SIMIAN LINE
IN BOTH HANDS

It is extremely rare to see the Simian line in both hands. When this does occur the subject tends to be way over the top emotionally. Everything is a drama and he will be madly in love one minute and insanely jealous the next.

Probably highly gifted, the person with two Simian lines lacks balance and can be very difficult to handle. Many of these types have an overwhelming need for secure material foundations and will work themselves into the ground in order to get the security they crave.

THE DOWNS SYNDROME HAND

The Downs syndrome hand is quite different from the hand with the Simian line. I have been following the case of Anita, a little Downs syndrome girl, since she was a tiny baby.

Soon after birth Anita's hand was podgy and broad with short little fingers. Where her Head and Heart lines should have been there was just a brief squiggle, like a disjointed cross in the centre of her palm.

But Anita thrived. Her parents gave her constant love, attention and stimulation and soon Anita was walking, talking and beginning to learn her letters.

As she grew, so did the lines in her palm. That peculiar little cross straightened into one, firmer line that lengthened gradually.

Today she is six years old and bright enough to attend an ordinary school. She reads, writes and copes with simple maths as well as her classmates. I'm quite sure that Anita has an excellent future.

IMPACT LINES

An impact line is found at the outside edge of the hand, close to the wrist. It rises up the palm towards the fourth finger of Mercury. Its presence indicates that someone important will soon come into the subject's life, turning it upside down.

There may be an unexpected romance, or perhaps a father figure or other influential person will appear and transform the subject's lifestyle.

If the impact line crosses a travel line it shows that the newcomer comes from abroad.

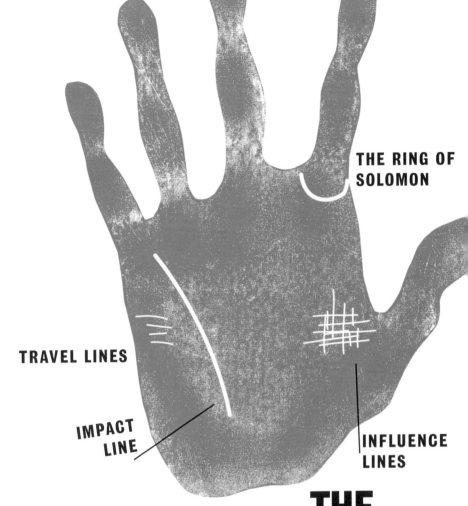

THE RING OF SOLOMON

TRAVEL LINES

IMPACT LINE

INFLUENCE LINES

TRAVEL LINES

These are short horizontal lines at the outside edge of the palm beneath the Heartline. Each line represents an important journey. The longer the line, the greater the distance likely to be travelled.

People with a great many travel lines will probably go overseas as part of their job.

A travel line that stretches across to the Success line or the Life line suggests that the subject might emigrate.

INFLUENCE LINES

These lines are found on the Mount of Venus, beneath the thumb, where they cling together in the form of a patchwork. When several of these lines actually touch the Life line, the subject is strongly influenced by his family.

A well patterned crisscross mark on the Mount of Venus unattached to the Life line suggests that the subject longs to influence others.

THE RING OF SOLOMON

The ring of Solomon is found at the base of the first finger of Jupiter, sweeping round in a curve towards the Life line. It shows that the subject is very impressionable and can be easily deceived or influenced by others. He is drawn to unusual things and people.

If the ring of Solomon is very pronounced and accompanied by a cross in the centre of the hand between the Head and Heart lines, it indicates that the subject may well be psychic.

THE QUADRANGLE

The area of the hand between the Heart and Head lines, excluding the Mount of Jupiter, is known as the Quadrangle. The size and appearance of the Quadrangle explains a great deal about the subject's attitude to life.

NARROW QUADRANGLE

If the gap between the Head and Heart lines is narrow, the subject is rather self-obsessed and takes little interest in the opinions of others. This individual thinks for himself and can be quite original, but he can also be rather bigoted.

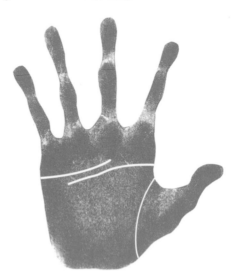

WIDE QUADRANGLE

When the gap between Head and Heart lines is wide, this suggests an extrovert, open-minded character with a good sense of humour. These types are generous and sympathetic, and tolerant of the opinions of others. If the palm is also springy, it shows that they can be easily hurt by unkind words.

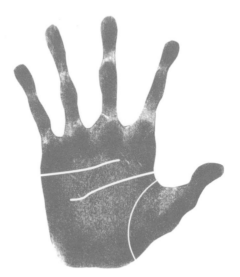

WIDENING QUADRANGLE

When the gap widens under the finger of Saturn it indicates that the subject is a disciplined self-starter. These types make their own way in the world with little help from others. I have seen self-made millionaires with this form of Quadrangle.

WIDENING QUADRANGLE

QUADRANGLE WIDENING UNDER APOLLO

The finger of Apollo usually brings good luck, and this case is no exception. When the Quadrangle widens under this finger, it suggests unexpected events leading to the fulfilment of an ambition.

A CROSS IN THE QUADRANGLE

When there is a clearly defined cross between the Heart and Head lines, it indicates that the subject is likely to be psychic. Even if they do not realize this they may have noticed that they have frequent "hunches" that turn out to be right.

A CROSS IN THE QUADRANGLE

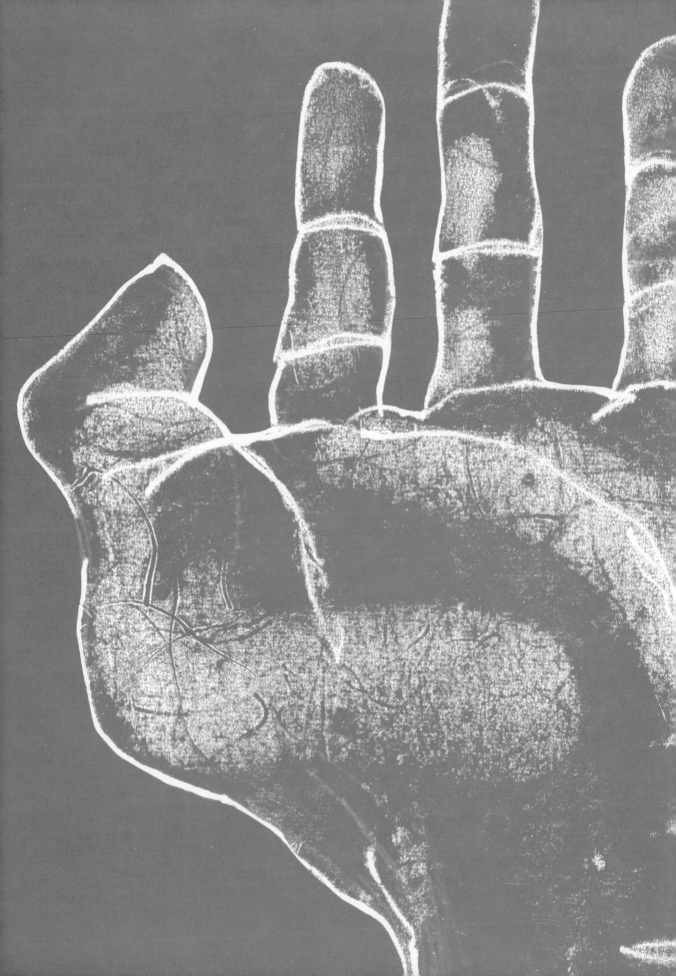

mounts

MOUNTS

As you work across the palm studying the individual lines, you may have noticed that the hand itself is not perfectly flat. There are raised, cushiony areas here and there, and these areas are often crisscrossed with their own little lines and marks. These small pads are known as the mounts. The most obvious mount, the Mount of Venus, has already been mentioned in the chapter on the thumb. The other four mounts lie beneath or slightly to the left of each finger. They take their names from the finger above them. The normal mount should be springy and well formed, obvious but not over-defined. In some hands, however, the mounts will be so flat as to be almost invisible, while in others they are positively overblown, giving the palm a spongy appearance. Like everything else in the hand, such details are important. Each type of mount has its own special significance.

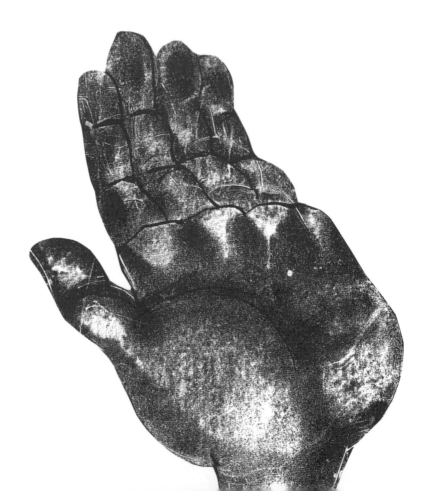

MARKS ON THE MOUNTS

When you have compared several different hands the chances are you will be amazed at the extraordinary differences there can be between palms. Leaving aside the more obvious variations in size and shape, the sheer number of lines on the palm can vary wildly.

Apart from the major lines, some hands are as smooth and clear as a blank sheet of paper, while others are a seething mass of tiny lines, crisscrossing and bisecting and branching off in all directions. This has nothing to do with age. I've seen septuagenarians with hands as smooth as a sixteen-year-old's and I've seen people in their twenties with palms as wrinkled as an old washerwoman's. In fact these tiny lines in the palm are determined by mental activity. Some people are full of nervous energy. Their minds are never still. They are constantly thinking and analysing, probing and questioning. They are nature's born worriers and their mental state shows itself on their palms in a frenetic network of lines.

The clearer the palm, the calmer the individual is likely to be. Most tiny worry lines need not be read individually, but a few are significant. They link together to form definite shapes with meanings of their own. These small symbols must be taken seriously.

There are five basic shapes found on the hand: crosses, stars, triangles, squares and little crisscross markings rather like a tiny portcullis which we call grilles.

Generally speaking, crosses are not a favourable sign. They suggest problems ahead. Stars and triangles are usually fortunate symbols; squares offer protection, and grilles are signs of stress and strain.

The precise meaning of these marks depends on their location. They can be anywhere on the palm, but are most commonly on the mounts.

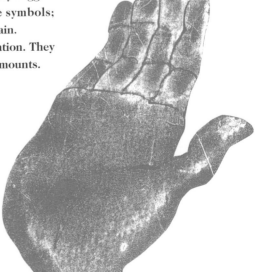

MOUNT OF JUPITER

NORMAL MOUNT

When this mount is well formed and neat it suggests a steady, law-abiding character with a strong sense of morality and deeply held religious beliefs.

FLAT MOUNT OF JUPITER

A flat mount is not such a good sign. It shows a lack of personal discipline, which could hinder the subject in her career. Unfortunately the flat mount also signifies a touch of arrogance, so the subject is unlikely to take advice or change her ways. When the flat mount is accompanied by a short Head line it suggests a dislike of authority.

OVER-DEVELOPED MOUNT OF JUPITER

When the mount is over-developed it indicates an ambitious nature, but not to the extent that the subject is likely to trample on others to reach the top. People with over-developed Mounts of Jupiter are also kind and considerate to others and like to help if they can.

MOUNT OF SATURN

NORMAL MOUNT OF SATURN

The person with the well formed Mount of Saturn is a doer. She is energetic, active and tends to have many hobbies and interests. These types are not great romantics, and career matters come before family and relationships.

FLAT MOUNT OF SATURN

A flat Mount of Saturn suggests a certain coldness in the character. There is a clinical approach to relationships, and sexually, these types tend to be rather selfish.

OVER-DEVELOPED MOUNT OF SATURN

When the Mount of Saturn is over-developed it shows a robust, earthy approach to sex. These subjects are not flirts, but they are unembarrassed about sexual matters and talk quite freely about their love lives. They have healthy physical appetites and see nothing wrong in indulging them.

MOUNT OF APOLLO

NORMAL MOUNT OF APOLLO

When this mount is nicely shaped and clearly defined it indicates a sociable individual who thoroughly enjoys the company of others. These types are well balanced and popular and also surprisingly good in an emergency.

FLAT MOUNT OF APOLLO

When this mount is flat, the subject tends to be lonely and finds it very difficult to get on with other people. He dislikes crowds and suffers from moodiness. Commonsense often deserts him and he feels unable to cope.

OVER-DEVELOPED MOUNT OF APOLLO

When this mount is very prominent it denotes great ambition allied to shrewdness and determination. If this type of mount is coupled with a strong Success line, the subject has just about everything he needs for a brilliant career.

MOUNT OF MERCURY

NORMAL MOUNT OF MERCURY

When the Mount of Mercury is well formed it shows that the subject is a good organizer with a strong sense of responsibility. These types enjoy money and the good things it can buy. They are not mean, but neither are they irresponsible. They must be careful of a tendency towards self-deception.

FLAT MOUNT OF MERCURY

Optimistic and flirty, the subject with a flat Mount of Mercury likes to have a good time without worrying about tomorrow. Unfortunately, she has a tendency to take offence very easily, often where none was intended, and for this reason frequently gets involved in quarrels.

OVER-DEVELOPED MOUNT OF MERCURY

When the Mount of Mercury is over-developed, it shows a broad-minded individual who is also very good with money. These types tend to have good business brains, and are also imaginative and creative.

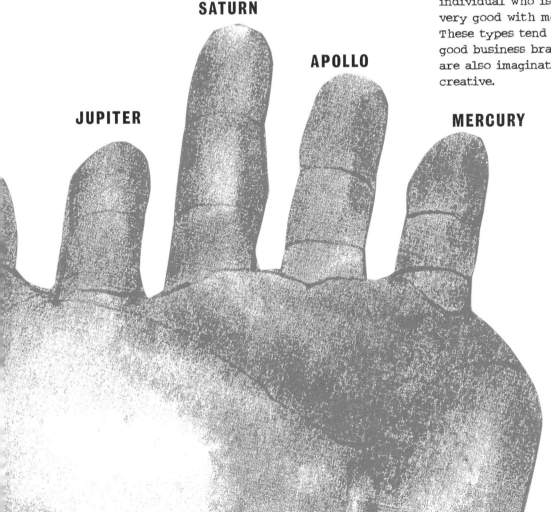

SATURN

APOLLO

JUPITER

MERCURY

CROSS

STAR

TRIANGLE

JUPITER

Crosses are not normally a fortunate sign, but on the Mount of Jupiter they are not at all unwelcome. In this location they suggest a happy surprise connected to a reunion of some kind, and the possibility of romance.

This is a wonderful symbol. It predicts dreams about to come true, accomplishments and an influx of money. It can even indicate fame and fortune.

This suggests a clever, highly diplomatic individual who will go far.

SATURN

A cross on this mount is a rather sinister sign. It suggests that someone with influence over the subject is dabbling in black magic.

Normally a star is a welcome sight, but on this mount it indicates losses, particularly of personal property. The subject should be particularly careful with bags, cameras, jewellery and other portable valuables.

A triangle is a good omen on this mount. It suggests something promising in the air - perhaps a new job, a new home or some other beneficial change.

APOLLO

This is not a pleasing symbol. It shows that the subject is too trusting for her own good. She is likely to be cheated or let down in some way.

This is a brilliant sign. A clearly marked star on the Mount of Apollo suggests money, fame and fortune could be on the way. A word of caution. This is a sign of wealth but not necessarily of happiness.

This is an interesting mark. It suggests that later in life, possibly in middle age, the subject will develop an apititude for art. It could even blossom into a second career.

MERCURY

If this cross stands out clearly it suggests the need for caution in business or career matters. There is deception around. All is not as it seems. Someone is not being honest with you and you need to find out why.

This mark denotes a fresh start. Now is the time to clear everything out of your life that you no longer need. This applies even to trivial domestic items that have outlived their usefulness.

This positive symbol suggests opportunities ahead. Be alert to take advantage of them.

SQUARE

GRILLE

ASCENDING LINES

Although it is not strictly a clearly defined mark, the free-standing vertical line uncon-nected to any other important line is frequently seen on the mounts. This type of marking is always a good sign.

JUPITER

When a square appears on this mount it indicates that the subject is about to receive a boost in his career. Promotion or a new job could be on the way.

If a grille appears on this mount the subject needs to be more tactful in his dealings with others. He is giving the impression of being vain and domi-neering.

When it appears on the Mount of Jupiter, it shows that there are better times ahead. A long cher-ished ambition could be about to be realized.

SATURN

The palmist is always fas-cinated to see a square on the Mount of Saturn. This rare marking indicates that the subject has heal-ing hands.

This is a strange sign. It suggests that the subject will be very tempted to make an unusual purchase. But beware, because the purchase is unwise in some way. It could well turn out to be stolen property.

One ascending line on this mount promises a finan-cial boost and happiness ahead. Several lines sug-gest that great good luck is on its way.

APOLLO

This is an auspicious sign for all businesses and partnerships. It suggests that the signing of papers is imminent and money will follow.

Losses in business are indicated and arguments are likely, probably as a result of the losses.

When these lines are well defined it suggests very good news indeed. Money and success imminent.

MERCURY

Usually this is a protec-tive symbol, but on the Mount of Mercury it is a warning. Caution is required in legal matters. Read all small print very carefully indeed.

Disappointments relating to money lie ahead. On the Mount of Mercury a grille suggests regrets over spending. Perhaps the sub-ject has spent too much or simply splashed out on an unwise purchase.

These welcome lines pre-dict good fortune and unexpected windfalls ahead.

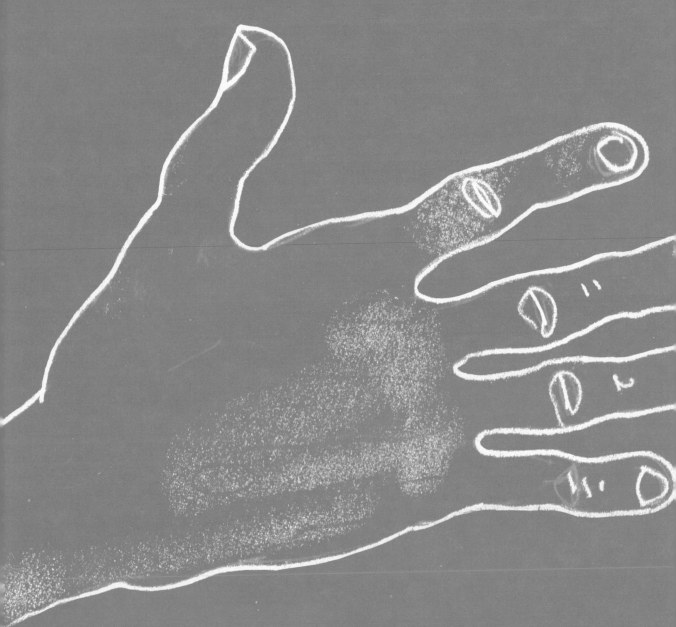

sex and

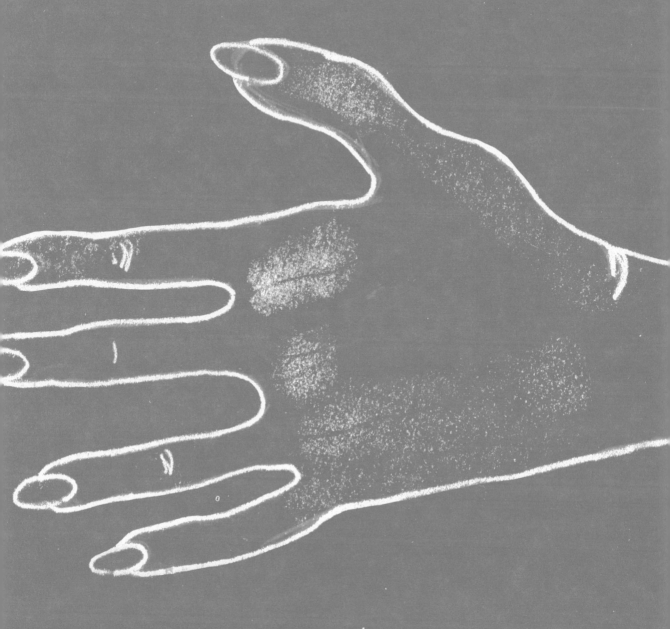

marriage

SEX AND MARRIAGE

I'm sure it comes as no surprise to learn that most young girls who visit me - and quite a few young men too - are particularly interested in one vital question. Or rather three vital questions that are all connected. Will they get married? Will they be happy? And how many children will they have?

Traditionally palmists have always been consulted on matters of love. Perhaps this is because love is the one area over which people feel they have no control. You cannot force yourself to fall in love. Neither can you persuade someone else to fall in love with you. It either happens or it doesn't, and the mechanism by which it works remains a complete mystery. And of course, even when you do fall in love there's no guarantee you will stay in love. Love can vanish as inexplicably as it appeared. Given that love is so vital to our happiness and sense of wellbeing, it's hardly surprising that over the centuries people have turned to palmists for a little guidance and reassurance in this difficult area.

These days palmistry is also widely used in many other areas of life. Businessmen and women in particular find it a valuable tool in building their businesses and developing their careers. Yet no matter how high up the tree they climb, very few people can remain indifferent to their love lives. From the chairman of the company to the youngest typist, we are all at the mercy of our emotions and those of the people we love. And this is why I think that for the forseeable future, questions about love and marriage will outweigh every other subject in my postbag.

THE MARRIAGE "M"

There is no such thing as a perfect marriage. We all have our ups and downs. Yet some couples do seem to have a happy knack of achieving a great many more ups than downs. It will be quite obvious to all their friends that these two really do have something special, but the happy couple is usually completely unable to explain what that is.

Their palms will tell a clearer story. In nine out of ten such cases I'm quite certain that you will see the marriage "M" bodly marked in the centre of their hands. Cup the hand, turn it slightly sideways, and in the hollow you will see that the Heart line, Head line and Life lines are linked by the Success line. The four lines run smoothly together to form a large letter "M" right across the palm.

This is a very fortunate sign, and it shows that no matter what problems the couple face, the union is blessed. They will be happy together.

More often than not a perfect letter "M" fails to appear. This is because the Success line is either not present at all, or because it reaches the Heart line too far down its course. This does not mean that the marriage is doomed. It simply shows that the couple will have to work harder and compromise more to achieve harmony.

MARRIAGE LINES

Many people are surprised to learn that marriage lines actually exist. They are found on the outside edge of the palm beneath the fourth finger of Mercury. They are small, horizontal lines reaching into the palm and they can best be seen by cupping the hand slightly, which deepens their appearance. Incidentally, such lines take no account of legal niceties. They don't necessarily indicate marriage in the legal sense, but they do show special long-term relationships in which the couple live together as man and wife.

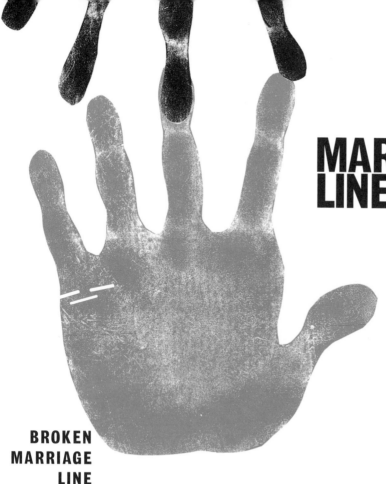

BROKEN MARRIAGE LINE

MORE THAN ONE LINE

Several faint lines followed by one deep line suggests a number of serious relationships, but only one marriage. Where there are two or more deep lines each line represents a new marriage. Quite often I see a small marriage line low on the mount and then another, longer line some distance above it right beneath the finger. This indicates a marriage when the subject was very young that failed to work, followed years later by a successful marriage.

Generally speaking, the higher up the mount the marriage line appears, the later in life that marriage is likely to be.

BROKEN MARRIAGE LINE

When the marriage line is broken it suggests a breakdown in the relationship, and unless great care is taken this could lead to divorce. However, a sister line often appears above the break to mend it, and this indicates that there will be a reconciliation.

PARALLEL MARRIAGE LINES

Sometimes two parallel marriage lines run side by side for a while, then join together to form a point. This sign is often found in the hands of service families and businessmen and women who work for long spells abroad. It shows a separation in the marriage due to circumstances outside the couple's control, but the relationship is none the worse for it.

ISLANDS ON THE MARRIAGE LINE

An island on the marriage line does not bode well. It indicates unfaithfulness.

CURVED MARRIAGE LINE

Occasionally you see a marriage line that curls round the base of the finger of Mercury in a definite semicircle. This denotes love at first sight that will blossom into marriage.

PARALLEL MARRIAGE LINES

CURVED MARRIAGE LINE

ISLANDS ON THE MARRIAGE LINE

THE PALM AND SEXUALITY

People often say that financial pressures cause the bulk of marriage breakdowns. Perhaps this is true. All I can say is that from the cases I encounter, it appears that sexual problems are the root cause of many divorces.

If I could sum up the basic difficulty, I would say that it was incompatibility of sexual needs. Sex is more important to some people than others, and some married people are bisexual or even homosexual but refuse to admit it to themselves or their partner. Sadly, too many couples fail to realize there is a problem until after the wedding. Yet if they had studied their hands and checked for incompatibility before they became deeply involved, they could have avoided a lot of heartache.

The girdle of Venus is a good indicator of physical appetites. It does not appear in every hand, but when it does, it is found in the form of a semi-circular line beneath the fingers but above the Heart line. Sometimes this line is a perfect semicircle, sometimes its course is broken into small pieces. All these marks are significant.

FULL GIRDLE OF VENUS

Passionate and steamy, subjects with a full girdle of Venus need an active sex life. As long as their partner is just as ardent, they will enjoy a successful and energetic relationship.

BROKEN GIRDLE OF VENUS

Strongly sensual, these types are restless and emotionally erratic. They can be moody, changeable and quick-tempered, but after a row they like to make up in bed.

NO GIRDLE OF VENUS

When there is no girdle of Venus, it suggests that passion does not feature largely in the subject's life. Although she may enjoy sex, it is not a strong need.

HIGHLY DEVELOPED GIRDLE OF VENUS

A very strong girdle suggests an individual who is constantly seeking variety. This may take the form of promiscuity but it can express itself in other ways. Drug addicts often have a deeply marked girdle of Venus. It is also found in the hand of rapists, although in these cases the Mount of Venus is markedly thin, indicating a cold, selfish nature.

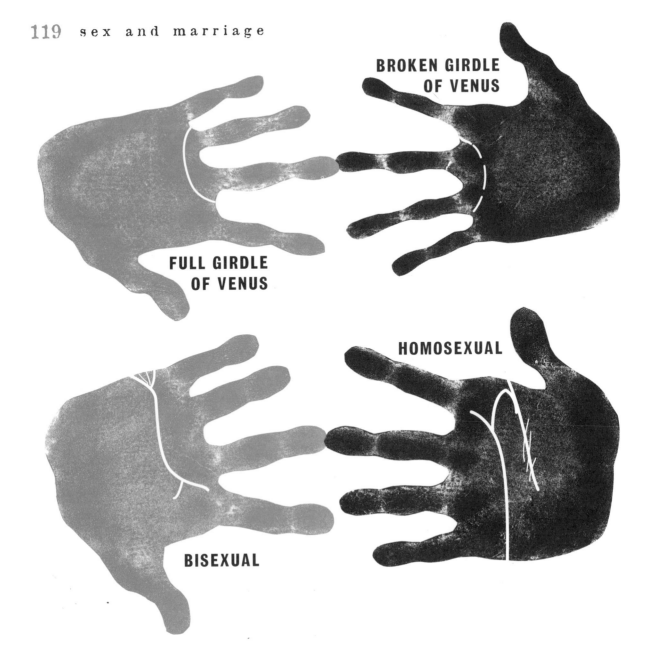

BROKEN GIRDLE OF VENUS

FULL GIRDLE OF VENUS

HOMOSEXUAL

BISEXUAL

BISEXUAL HANDS

A bisexual nature can be detected in the Heart line. In a bisexual man, the Heart line starts crisscrossed with tiny lines in the shape of a fan, and ends in two prongs, one pointing up to the fingers, the other down to the Head line. The bisexual woman has a similar Heart line, except that the fan at the beginning is replaced by an island.

HOMOSEXUAL HANDS

Homosexuality, both male and female, is indicated when the Heart line ends in a pronounced fork, with the lower prong pointing towards the Head line, then turning back on itself like a fish hook. Since unacknowledged homosexuality often causes a great deal of stress, the hands are likely to be covered with tiny worry lines and there could be grilles across the Heart line.

THE PALM AND PARENTHOOD

In some hands the presence of children is strongly marked from the beginning. In others the signs do not appear until the baby is actually on its way. The child line is a small vertical line on the Mount of Mercury, close to the marriage line and pointing up towards the finger. The number of lines predicts the number of children the subject can expect. Short deep lines indicate girls; long deep lines suggest boys. Two lines joined together denote twins.

A star on a child line suggests that the child may well become famous. The absence of child lines does not mean that the subject will be childless. It may simply be that the lines have not yet formed. However, when there are no lines present there is another factor to check: the bracelets (sometimes called the racelettes) at the base of the hand around the wrist. There may be one, two or even three bracelets forming a semicircle around the inside of the wrist. One smooth bracelet indicates physical strength. Two bracelets are a welcome sign, denoting good health. Three bracelets are especially lucky, showing that health, happiness and comfort are in store. The bracelets also give valuable information about whether a subject will have children. And to find out what sort of family life lies ahead, you can examine the "family ring" at the base of the thumb.

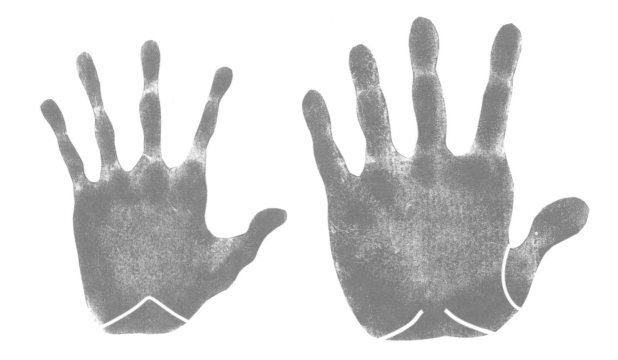

THE ARCHED BRACELET

When the bracelet nearest the hand rises into an arch in the centre that points into the palm, it suggests that the marriage will probably be childless, particularly if there are no child lines present on the Mount of Mercury.

BROKEN FIRST BRACELET

Difficulties with a pregnancy are indicated. Care must be taken to avoid miscarriage. However, if there is a sister line or strong child lines present on the Mount of Mercury, it shows that the subject will have a healthy baby in the end.

If the first bracelet is broken, with one half linked to the Life and Success lines, this suggests a surprise pregnancy. Not every woman actually wants children, but when this type of bracelet is present the subject is likely to be in for a big surprise.

THE FAMILY RING

This is not a true ring, but a semicircle that clasps the base of the second phalange (bone) of the thumb at the point where it joins the hand. From inside, it has the appearance of a ring.

When the ring is deep and clear it suggests strong family ties.

When there is more than one ring present it shows either a difficult childhood, or that when the subject becomes a parent he will find life more difficult than he thought.

A chained family ring is quite common. This indicates difficulties or problems in the family.

CASE HISTORY
A MARRIAGE LATER IN LIFE

When Marsha came to see me she was beginning to despair. She was a smart, attractive woman in her mid-thirties and she ran a successful PR company. She arrived in an expensive sports car, she had recently bought herself a new house and she was planning the holiday of a lifetime - a trip to the Seychelles.

Marsha had done extremely well, but the acquisition of all these lovely things had not brought her the pleasure she expected. She told me she would give it all up, if she could find the right man and settle down.

Privately I doubted this. Marsha's elegant hands showed that she enjoyed the good things in life, and her determined thumb and strong Head line indicated an aptitude for business. I felt she would greatly miss all these things if she abandoned her career.

I examined Marsha's palm. Just above the Heart line beneath the fourth finger of Mercury was a short marriage line. Then there was a large, blank space and high up, almost at the base of the finger, was another strong marriage line. I asked Marsha if she had been married before and she confessed that at eighteen she had married her childhood sweetheart, mainly to get away from her strict parents. Predictably, the couple were too young to settle down. A year later they split up, and that was when Marsha threw herself into her career.

"I thought I'd never want to get married again," said Marsha. "But now I'd really like to settle down."

I was able to reassure her that she would find a good man and that a successful marriage was destined to come later in life.

Five years went by, then out of the blue one morning I received a wedding invitation. Marsha had fallen in love with the director of one of the companies who used her PR firm. They had a whirlwind romance and were married three months later.

Whirlwind romances can be very risky of course, but in this case, judging from the length and strength of the marriage line, I think it will work out very well.

CASE HISTORY

A LONGED-FOR BABY

I remember a young woman who came to see me. She was pleasant and cheerful until I happened to ask if she was pregnant. Suddenly she burst into tears.

Apparently she and her husband had been married ten years and had been trying to start a family throughout. They had had no luck, and were beginning to fear that they would never have a child.

Yet I had asked about the pregnancy because I could see quite clearly on the woman's Mount of Mercury the beginnings of a newly formed child line, the sort of line that often appears after conception. It looked to me like a female line.

The woman didn't think she was pregnant, but she rushed off to buy a pregnancy testing kit. A couple of hours later she telephoned in high excitement. The test was positive. She couldn't believe it, because it seemed that after all this time she was expecting a baby.

Nine months later her husband contacted me with the good news. After a trouble-free pregnancy, they were now the proud parents of a beautiful little girl.

A SURPRISE PREGNANCY

Claire came to see me in some indignation. She had just discovered she was pregnant. She liked children and enjoyed playing with her friends' babies, but she was not at all sure she wanted a family of her own. She had a fulfilling career, several pets and a happy relationship with her husband. They enjoyed life just as it was.

Claire had read about the child lines in a palmistry book. Finding none on her own palm, she assumed she would never have a family.

Underneath all this protest, I sensed that Claire was really thrilled about this extraordinary accident. When I looked at her hand I saw a tiny child just starting to appear on the Mount of Mercury. More to the point, the first bracelet at the base of her hand was broken in two, one side stopping halfway across her palm, the other curling round her Life line to join up with her Success line. A very faint sister line linked them all together. It was quite obvious that no matter what she planned, she was destined to fall pregnant.

When Claire's little daughter arrived, she fell madly in love with her. Claire and her husband turned out to be devoted parents.

CASE HISTORY

CASE HISTORY

ENDNOTE

Now you have got to the end of the book you should have learned a great many things about reading palms. You probably know more than you realize. Of course this knowledge is of no use until you put it into practice, and the next step is to study a genuine hand. Don't be impatient or too hard on yourself. You can't expect to produce an expert reading on your first attempt, but the more hands you study, the more accurate you will become.

Here are a few thoughts to help you before you begin. As I've made clear, both hands must be studied for a successful reading. Lines may be present in one hand and absent from the other. Or the two hands may show different formations altogether. In addition, fingers, thumbs and mounts may show surprising differences. So do remember to study both hands and weigh up your findings carefully before giving the analysis. Take your time. If you need to check a detail with this book, mark your place so that you can go back to it quickly if necessary.

Occasionally you may find signs in a hand that are not particularly favourable or flattering. Take care. There is a chance that you have read them incorrectly. Go back and recheck. If you are quite sure that your impressions are accurate, use great tact and diplomacy when you relay them to the subject. Obviously if you see some problem approaching of which the subject should be warned, he or she will want to know. But never forget that some people are nervous and easily frightened. Couch your warning very carefully and be as positive as possible. Before you begin, you might like to test yourself on the depth of your knowledge. I have not provided answers to the questions opposite, so there is no temptation to cheat! The answers are all contained in the preceding pages. If you don't know them, you need to read the relevant chapters again. On pages 126 and 127 you will find photocopies of two real handprints. See what you can discover about them and then check with my interpretations.

1 Name two of the basic hand shapes.

2 What is the third phalange of the thumb?

3 Can you get a good reading with one hand only?

4 Name the three major lines of the hand.

5 What hand shape is associated with a good sportsman or woman?

6 What is the difference between the major and the minor hands?

7 Where would you find the girdle of Venus?

8 Is a clammy hand a good sign?

9 Why are the hands of twins different?

10 What does it mean to have pointed hands?

11 If you were in the middle of reading this book could you give a perfect reading?

12 Where would you look for signs of success?

13 What does a fork at the end of the Head line signify?

14 Where would you find the travel lines?

The main points to notice about this hand are the square, regular shape, the slight curve to the edge of the palm and the fairly straight Heart line. This indicates that the subject is level-headed and would be good in business. That slight curve to the palm also shows some sort of talent.

There is a wide gap between the Heart and Head lines showing that this is an individual with a good sense of humour and there is what looks like a fork a the end of the Head line which could suggest a gift for writing.

Unfortunately, the Success line stops at the Head line, showing that career progress has been blocked in some way and in the lower part of the palm there are lots of tiny random lines. This is a sign of stress and nervous tension.

It could be that the owner of this hand lacks confidence and because of this, has not been able to achieve his or her potential.

Here we have the classic Simian line I mentioned in an earlier chapter — this is the feature which combines the Heart and Head lines into one line which slashes across the hand from one side of the palm to the other.

Assuming that it appears in one hand only, it shows a highly intelligent person, and coupled with the wide curve on the outside of the palm, I would say that this individual has a wonderful creative talent of some kind.

Those telltale criss cross lines all over the palm, however, show that the subject is a born worrier.

There are also a lot of travel lines on the edge of the palm, suggesting that despite his or her anxious nature, this is a person who will move around a lot, particularly abroad.

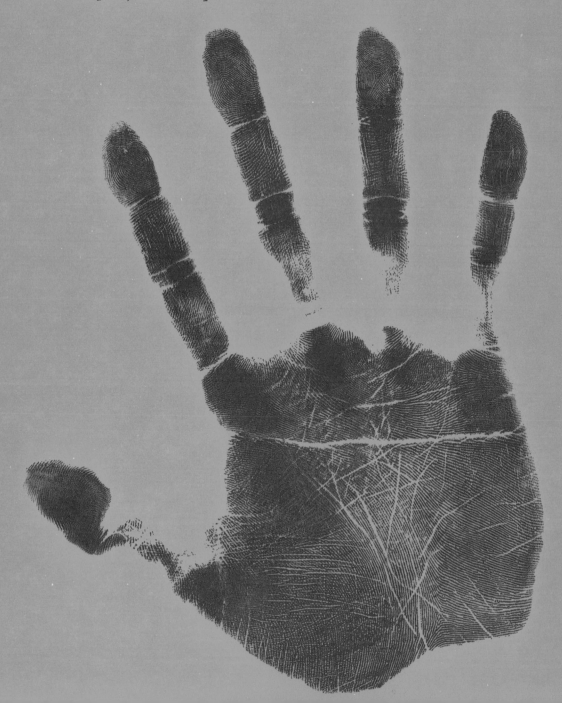

index